The Great
WHALESHIP DISASTER
of 1871

The Great
WHALESHIP DISASTER
of 1871

Julie Baker

MORGAN
REYNOLDS
PUBLISHING

Greensboro, North Carolina

THE GREAT WHALESHIP DISASTER OF 1871
Copyright © 2007 by Julie Baker

Library of Congress Cataloging-in-Publication Data

Baker, Julie, 1967-
  The great whaleship disaster of 1871 / by Julie Baker.
     p. cm.
  Includes bibliographical references and index.
  ISBN-13: 978-1-59935-043-1
  ISBN-10: 1-59935-043-2
  1. Henry Taber (Whaleship) 2. Shipwrecks--Arctic Ocean. 3. Survival
after airplane accidents, shipwrecks, etc. 4. Packard, Timothy C. I. Title.
  G530.H3975B35 2007
  910.9163'27--dc22

                                        2007002807

Printed in the United States of America
First Edition

To Frank, Ashley and Lauren

Contents

Chapter One:
September 12, 1871 11

Chapter Two:
Leaving New Bedford 14

Chapter Three:
Captain and Crew 27

Chapter Four:
Life At Sea 40

Chapter Five:
The Floating Factory 51

Chapter Six:
Troubles in the Pacific 64

Chapter Seven:
Gathering of the Arctic Fleet 69

Chapter Eight:
Early Warning 79

Chapter Nine:
Whales and Ice 89

Chapter Ten:
Shipwrecked 98

Chapter Eleven:
Homeward Bound 116

Timeline 129
Sources 131
Bibliography 137
Web sites 140
Index 142

Whaleship
(Courtesy of Bridgeman Art Library)

one
September 12, 1871

O n September 12, 1871, Captain Timothy C. Packard gave his last official commands as master of the whaleship *Henry Taber*. He ordered the *Taber*, although it was in excellent sailing condition and loaded with a valuable cargo of whale oil and baleen, to be abandoned off the frigid northwest coast of Alaska, thousands of miles from a friendly port. He then ordered the *Taber's* three dozen crewmen into small, wooden boats and told them to row southbound through seventy miles of narrow channels in a frozen sea. He could not guarantee their survival.

Unfortunately, the orders were not unique to Captain Packard and his beleaguered crew. Thirty-one other whaleship masters, the most experienced, respected commanders on the high seas, had found it necessary to order their men to take the same risky course of action.

Months earlier, the commanders had sailed their ships into Arctic waters, as they did every year, in a loosely organized fleet to pursue migrating bowhead whales. They had expected to work in the far northern reaches of the globe until October, when the weather would become too cold and stormy.

But in 1871, winter arrived early. September brought violent winds and strong currents, forcing miles of solid ice toward shore, where the thirty-two whaleships were anchored. Three of the vessels were completely crushed, and the twenty-nine others were surrounded by ice, unable to flee to safety. More than 1,200 men, three captains' wives, and five young children were suddenly confronted with a nine-month long Arctic winter. With only enough food and heat-fuel to sustain them for ninety days, they had to abandon the ships or die of starvation and exposure.

But where would they go? And what about the financial losses caused by the abandonment? Even if the worried captains somehow managed to save every life entrusted to their commands, leaving the unprecedented number of seaworthy vessels behind would draw harsh criticism from whaling investors around the world.

As a symbol of unity to silence future critics, the commanders drafted a letter detailing the situation and their uneasy, but unanimous, decision to leave their ships. On September 12, they met for the final time to sign the document.

Winds rattled the towering rigging of the whaleship *Florida* where the commanders met. Massive chunks of ice passed near the *Florida's* wooden hull as Captain Packard hoisted himself out of his small boat and onto the ship's deck. He crossed to the hatch and climbed down from the crisp Arctic cold into the moldy air of the ship's dark cabin below.

The handwritten letter he and the other captains had come to sign lay on the table in the center of the dimly lit room. A few men scribbled their names to the bottom of it and hurried away. Others lingered before signing, perhaps in the hope that a last-minute miracle would make it unnecessary.

As ice creaked and crushed outside the *Florida's* warm refuge, Captain Packard added his name to the bottom of the page. Then he ascended the ship's ladder once more to confront their uncertain future.

two
Leaving
New Bedford

Before the discovery of petroleum and the widespread use of plastics, oil and baleen obtained from whales provided many products important to the comfort of people and productivity of factories. Throughout the nineteenth century, whale oil was used to light homes and businesses. It also served as a lubricant for the massive machinery of the thriving Industrial Revolution. Whale baleen (called "bone" by whalemen) consists of the long strips that hang from the upper jaws of some whales. A strong, flexible material, baleen was used by nineteenth-century manufacturers in the production of many items, including umbrella tines, fishing rods, and women's hoop skirts. The worldwide whaling industry was big business.

Dependence on whales dates back as far as the Stone Age. Images of early hunters carrying crude harpoons, sailing in small boats, and engaging in life-and-death battles with the giant mammals are depicted on numerous ancient rock

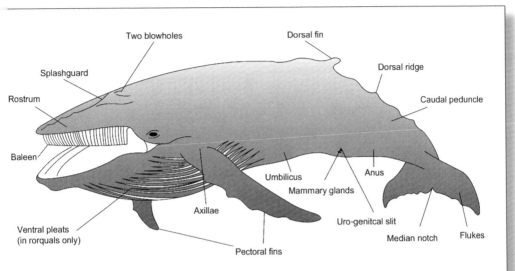

Baleen Whale (Mysticeti) Physical Characteristics

carvings. But it was the men from the northeastern United States in the 1800s that transformed the endeavor of whaling from individual, small-scale undertakings into a centralized, major economic enterprise. At its peak, the American whaling industry involved hundreds of ships, thousands of sailors, tens of thousands of small businesses, and spanned all of the world's oceans.

By the middle of the nineteenth century, whaling had become the fifth-largest industry in the United States. It contributed $10 million annually to the nation's economy and employed more than 60,000 workers at sea and on land. New Englanders, particularly those in the state of Massachusetts, owned and commanded almost 80 percent of all whaleships. Nowhere were whaling dollars more appreciated than in the coastal Massachusetts town of New Bedford.

The New Bedford harbor *(Library of Congress)*

Located fifty miles south of Boston, New Bedford was the central point of departure and arrival for most American whaling ventures. The town was one of the wealthiest communities per capita in the world and its 20,000 residents owed the status to their whalers' successes at sea, and to income generated by local businesses when ships returned to port. Shipbuilders, coopers, sailmakers, outfitters, provisioners, cordage manufacturers, and sparmakers catered to demands of whaling investors, ships, and crews. Boardinghouses, hotels, bakeries, tailors, banks, schools, and churches flourished from the steady influx of whaling money and men.

Herman Melville sailed out of New Bedford in 1841 aboard the whaleship *Acushnet*. In his famous novel *Moby Dick*, set largely aboard a whaling ship, he describes New Bedford as

Herman Melville wrote about New Bedford in the novel *Moby Dick*.
(Library of Congress)

"the dearest place to live in all New England" and remarks
on the opulence and grandeur of the town's homes and gardens: "All these brave houses and flowery gardens came
from the Atlantic, Pacific, and Indian Oceans. One and all,

they were harpooned and dragged up hither from the bottom of the sea."

Melville would still have recognized New Bedford's wharf in 1868, almost three decades after he departed from it. Horse-drawn carriages still clopped over uneven cobblestones as dockworkers struggled to unload heavy casks of whale oil from ships' holds. Languages from Portugal, Germany, the South Pacific, and the West Indies were still heard over shouts and laughter of men as they spread clingy wet seaweed over the oil casks to protect from shrinkage in the day's bright sunlight. Clanging blacksmiths' hammers and banging coopers' mallets rang out as sails, spars, and barrels of water were stacked along the wharf. The smell of sea salt, ripening fruits, burning tobacco, frying food, and melting tar still swirled in the heavy air. And, as always in New Bedford, the strong stench of whale oil permeated everything.

Melville had sailed out of New Bedford just as the whaling industry was approaching its peak years. During the second half of the nineteenth century the depletion of the whale population, the American Civil War, and the discovery of petroleum had diminished the whaling industry. With each passing year, fewer men signed on to work whaleships, and fewer vessels departed New Bedford's harbor. Ships that did set sail had to travel farther and be absent from home longer in order to earn a profit. Many ship commanders ventured into the dangerous waters of the poorly charted Arctic Ocean to fill their holds with oil and bone. One such vessel was the whaling bark *Henry Taber*.

The three-masted *Taber* had been built in 1855 and weighed 296 tons, was 107 feet in length, just under twenty-eight feet in width, and seventeen feet in depth. In the summer of 1868, it was one of several ships docked at New Bedford's harbor being readied for an Arctic-bound voyage.

At a time when the average land-based manufacturing company was worth about $5,000, a single whaling venture cost more than $20,000 to outfit and supply. Such expense normally required several investors. Merchants, sailors, carpenters, riggers, doctors, bakers, jewelers—anyone with a few dollars to spare—could invest in an outgoing voyage in the hope of receiving a share of profits upon a ship's return.

Taber, Gordon & Company owned the *Henry Taber*. The company was a partnership consisting of several New Bedford wholesale grocers and ship chandlers. Ship chandlers sold supplies and equipment to sailing vessels. From *Taber, Gordon & Company*'s headquarters on the corner of Front Street at Central Wharf, arrivals and departures of whaling vessels were carefully tracked.

No money was made when a whaleship idled in port, and the seven businessmen of *Taber, Gordon & Company* were determined to send the *Taber* to sea again as soon as possible. An agent for the company ordered an inspection of the ship's hull to insure it was free of leaks and wear before it sailed. The enormous vessel was laid on its side, "hove down," to expose any damage on its underside. Carpenters stripped away the copper and pine sheathing to expose seams in the ship's planking and pounded in new oakum caulking. The ship's underside was then covered with hot tar and tar paper. Pine planks were hammered over the hull and copper sheets were attached to cover everything below the ship's waterline. It was tedious, important work, but investors knew that thorough maintenance performed on the ship in New Bedford would prevent wasted time on repairs at foreign ports.

THE WHALE FISHERY.

Whale-ships at New Bedford wharves; ship hove down for repairs; oil-casks. (Sect. v, vol. ii, pp. 289, 290)

From a photograph by U. S. Fish Commission.

A ship "hove down" for repairs (*Courtesy of the National Oceanic and Atmospheric Administration*)

When satisfied the *Taber* was again seaworthy, the agent ordered the huge ship restored to an upright position. Its webs of masts, spars, and rigging were then inspected and replaced, where needed. Everything on board was repainted except for the decks, which were holystoned, or scrubbed, by scouring large blocks of sandstone over the wood. The ship's sails and equipment were checked and secured.

A stevedore was hired to oversee the loading process for the *Taber*. Under his watchful eye workers lugged heavy barrels

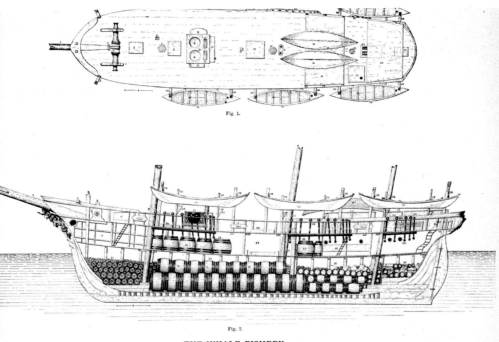

Fig. 1.

Fig. 2.

THE WHALE FISHERY.

Deck plan and sectional plan of whaling bark Alice Knowles, of New Bedford, Mass. (Sect. v, vol. ii, p. 234.)

Drawing by C. S. Raleigh.

[See explanation opposite.]

PLATE 169

This diagram shows the interior of a whaleship filled with barrels of whale oil, bundles of baleen, and supplies for the crew aboard.
(Courtesy of the National Oceanic and Atmospheric Administration)

of water into the hold. Unassembled oil casks, to be built at sea when actual whaling began, were carefully stacked below deck. Enough food and supplies were delivered to sustain the ship's thirty-two crew members for several months.

Melville wrote, "Everyone knows what a multitude of things—beds, saucepans, knives and forks, shovels and tongs, napkins, nut-crackers, and what not, are indispensable to the business of housekeeping. Just so with whaling, which necessitates a three-years' housekeeping upon the wide ocean, far from all grocers, coster-mongers, doctors, bakers, and bankers."

While the *Taber* underwent its final preparations, the agent hired the ship's officers and crew. The *Taber's* size required it to have a captain, three officers (also known as "mates"), at least four boatsteerers, a cooper, cook, steward, carpenter, and enough men to handle its massive sails and whaleboats. Additional crewmen would be added in Honolulu before the ship journeyed into the Arctic.

Captain Timothy C. Packard, age thirty-three was hired as the *Taber's* commander. Packard's resume was impressive. He had sailed on whaleships since he was fifteen years old, rising in rank from greenhand to seaman to officer. He had sailed on at least two occasions in the coveted role of ship's captain. On voyages spanning the globe, he had proven to be an expert sailor, a dependable navigator, a courageous whaler, and a strong manager of men. Married with two small children (Fanny, age four, and Timothy Jr., age one), Packard had returned that summer from commanding the bark *Andrews* to the North Atlantic and was available for the *Taber's* upcoming five-year voyage.

John Stivers, age forty-two, was hired as the *Taber's* first mate. As second-in-command of the ship, Stivers would be in charge of insuring Captain Packard's orders were carried out, maintaining discipline among the crewmembers, keeping the ship's official log book, and managing navigational duties. George Payne, age twenty-eight, and Alexander Omey, age twenty-two, were hired as second and third mates. The three officers would take turns managing the daily tasks of supervising the crew and standing watch on deck. When a whale was spotted, each mate would command his own whaleboat in pursuit.

Everyone on the crew would share daily chores and assist in the hunting and processing of whales, but several jobs on the ship required men who possessed specialized skills. Boatsteerers, or "harpooners," (a term never used by whalemen) were hired to maneuver the whaleboats during a whale chase and to inflict the dangerous first attack upon the animal. Captain Packard's twenty-two-year-old brother-in-law, Warren Bullock, was signed on as one of the *Taber's* four boatsteerers, along with Banabas Robinson, George Wood, and twenty-eight-year-old Abram Briggs.

The ship's coopers, Heinrich Benecke and Paul Schimdt, would make and repair oil casks. The ship's steward, John Ellis, was to assist the captain and serve meals to the officers. Henry Peterson, the *Taber's* carpenter, would make required repairs to the ship and whaleboats during the long months at sea. David Edwards, shipkeeper, would handle the *Taber* when the captain and officers left the ship to chase whales. Edward Gibbin was signed on as the ship's cook. Ordinary sailors were hired to handle the sails, climb the rigging, make knots, hunt whales, and process blubber and bone. Five crewmen had experience on whaleships, and at least three had sailed on prior voyages with Captain Packard.

But for twelve men on the *Taber's* outbound crew, the 1868 expedition would be their first experience on a whaleship. These men were called "greenhands" and would be given simpler jobs until they could assume tasks with more responsibility. One of their first priorities would be to learn the names and functions of nearly ten miles of ropes used to control the vessel at sea.

Regardless of individual variations in skill, the crewmembers would be expected to work as a team. Everyone's role was vital to the ship's safety and profitability.

A total of thirty-two crewmen were listed on the *Henry Taber's* shipping papers filed by *Taber, Gordon & Company.* Half of them were twenty-five years old or younger. Seventeen were from the United States (mostly New England) and seven were from Germany. The rest listed their home countries as Belgium, Denmark, England, and the West Indies.

As was the custom in New Bedford at the time, the agent probably arranged for the men to have room and board while awaiting the October sail date. The costs of accommodations would be deducted from each man's pay at the end of the voyage.

It was also customary for seamen to receive an advance on their potential pay prior to setting sail in order to buy necessary clothing and toiletries for the long journey. The amounts varied depending upon the man's job. Cabin boys could receive around twenty-five dollars in advance, ordinary seamen about forty dollars, boatsteerers approximately seventy, and mates anywhere from one hundred to three hundred dollars. A captain might receive up to five hundred dollars before his first day on the job. All advance money given to the men was carefully detailed on company ledgers and would be deducted from their final pay when the ship returned to port.

Whalemen did not receive a paycheck at the end of their work week or month. Instead, they received a percentage, called a "lay." The lay was specified in advance of the ship's sailing and depended on the total net proceeds earned upon the voyage's completion. The lay received depended upon the generosity of the ship's owners and the man's skill level. Captain Packard agreed to command the *Henry Taber* for 1/15 of any profits collected at the end of the ship's planned five-year journey. If his years at sea resulted in financial gain (after deducting costs of the venture and owners' shares) of $15,000, for example, the captain could expect to receive $1,000. His advance would be subtracted from this amount, of course, as well as any personal expenses incurred during the voyage.

First mate John Stivers signed on to be second-in-command of the *Taber* for 1/21 lay. The second and third mates agreed to sail for 1/32 and 1/58, respectively. Abram Briggs, initially hired as a boatsteerer, signed on for 1/95 of the profits.

If the ship made money and if a seaman returned with the vessel—neither of these conditions were guaranteed—he was typically paid in cash. Occasionally men were paid with casks of the oil they had worked to obtain, which they could turn around and sell. While the *Taber's* owners had agreed to pay the ship's cabin boy in lay wages at the end of the voyage (1/250), some whaleship contracts only guaranteed cabin boys "clothes" or "board" as their entire pay for several years' work.

The men understood that if they did not find any whales during the ship's time at sea, they would not receive any pay, even if they had worked for a year. If the *Taber* was lost at sea during its voyage, those surviving the shipwreck would not get paid for any oil or bone lost on board during the wreck, regardless of the amount of time or effort they had invested in obtaining the valuable cargo. If a seaman decided to quit his job without permission of the ship's captain, he forfeited everything.

It was raining at 9:30 a.m. on October 22, 1868, when Captain Packard and the New Bedford harbor pilot finally rowed out to the *Taber* where it was anchored off Clark's Point. Fully stocked with provisions and crew, the ship was ready to begin its voyage around the world.

The following day, favorable winds allowed the pilot to maneuver the bulky vessel to open sea. Once he had taken it safely away from all land-based hazards, the harbor pilot left the *Taber*, climbed back into his boat, and returned to port alone. Captain Packard noted in his log that "with a beautiful breeze, stowed away our anchors and chains, washed our decks" and steered towards the south-southeast. The *Henry Taber*, white sails unfurled to catch fresh autumn winds, was underway.

three
Captain and Crew

Within the first hours at sea, Captain Packard called all hands on deck, and the new crew assembled for his post-departure briefing. He introduced himself as commander of the *Henry Taber* and reminded his men of the importance of working together to ensure the journey would be profitable. As master of the ship, Captain Packard would hold final authority over every aspect of each man's life while at sea. He expected complete, unquestioned compliance to all of his orders. Anyone who rebelled, by acts of insubordination, desertion, or attempted mutiny, would be severely punished.

With the captain's briefing accomplished, first mate John Stivers assigned the men into two groups for "watch" duties. A watch was a division of time on board the ship. There were seven watches in a twenty-four-hour period. Five were four hours each, and two (called dog watches) took place from 4 to 6 p.m. and from 6 to 8 p.m. The sailors, divided into two

THE LOOK-OUT. A.

An illustration of a whaler in the masthead, on the lookout for whales
(Reproduced with the permission of the copyright owner, Imperial Tobacco, UK)

watch groups, would alternate work schedules, leaving one watch on deck while the other was off duty below.

Each man was also assigned to work two hours at the masthead each day and two hours at the ship's helm. The masthead was a lookout position located approximately one hundred feet above the deck of the *Taber*. A man positioned high in the rigging could constantly scan the seas for whales, land or other ships.

"In most American whale[ships] the mast-heads are manned almost simultaneously with the vessel's leaving her port," Melville wrote, "even though she may have fifteen thousand miles, and more, to sail ere reaching her proper cruising ground. And if, after three . . . years' voyage she is drawing nigh home with anything empty in her . . . then, her mast-heads are kept manned to the last . . . [in] the hope of capturing one whale more."

Before dismissing the men to their new shipboard duties, Stivers divided the sailors into additional groups of six men each to crew the *Taber's* whaleboats during whale chases. Each officer chose a boatsteerer who would be responsible for directing the course of the boats during each whale chase, and for harpooning the enormous animals. The captain and mates would serve as "boatheaders," responsible for the ultimate safety of their crews and for inflicting the fatal strike against any whale the boatsteerer successfully managed to wound. The other four men assigned to each boat would row under the boatheaders' directions.

With Stivers competently attending the *Taber's* organizational needs on deck, Captain Packard went below to his quarters to chart the ship's course. Many New Bedford captains, bound for the Pacific Ocean, navigated their vessels in the direction of the infamous Cape Horn, at the tip of South America. The passage offered whalers the fastest route to whaling grounds, but there was a potentially deadly price to pay for the luxury of speed. Winds at Cape Horn could reach one hundred miles per hour, and waves were often reported

Although many whaling captains used the quicker but more dangerous route around the tip of South America to get to the Arctic, Captain Packard decided to sail on the safer route around Africa's Cape of Good Hope.

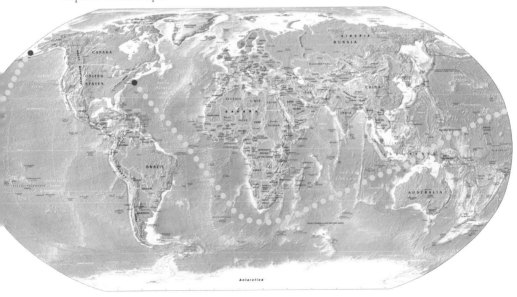

at heights of sixty feet. Countless ships had been smashed against the rocky South American coastline or blown off course toward the hull-slashing icebergs of Antarctica.

Captain Packard opted instead to navigate the *Taber* on a more predictable route to the south-southeast around Africa's Cape of Good Hope. The navigational decision would necessitate crossing the Atlantic and Indian Oceans prior to reaching the whaling grounds of the Pacific, but would offer more favorable sailing conditions.

The first days at sea were especially difficult on the *Taber's* greenhand sailors. Unaccustomed to a ship's movement on ocean swells, debilitating sea sickness plagued many. Ten days into the *Taber's* voyage, five men were noted on the ship's sick list. But sick or not, they were expected to fulfill their duties to the extent possible. The rigging had to be attended, the sails always needed to be furled or unfurled, and the whaleboats had to be maintained.

It did not take long to transform the bewildered greenhands into competent sailors who knew how to square the yards, reef the sails, climb the rigging, scrub the deck, and care for whaling equipment. Harpoons, lances, and knives were sharpened, and the whale line was coiled. And, as always, lookouts were posted in the masts high above the ship's deck in case a whale could be spotted anywhere in the ship's vicinity.

The routine tasks were learned a week and a half into the voyage and the focus of the greenhands' education switched to the care and use of the whaleboats. Four of the *Taber's* whaleboats were securely attached to the ship's exterior sides and kept in a constant state of readiness. These slender boats were nearly thirty feet long and six feet wide. They were

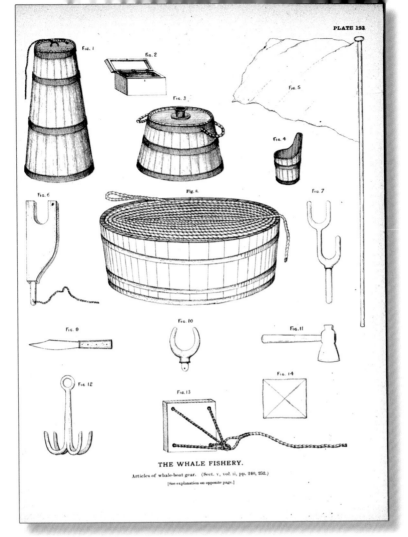

PLATE 193

Fig. 1
Fig. 2
Fig. 3
Fig. 5
Fig. 4
Fig. 6
Fig. 8
Fig. 7
Fig. 9
Fig. 10
Fig. 11
Fig. 12
Fig. 14
Fig. 13

THE WHALE FISHERY.

Articles of whale-boat gear. (Sect. v, vol. ii, pp. 240, 252.)

[See explanation on opposite page.]

Items commonly found on whaleboats (*Courtesy of the National Oceanic and Atmospheric Administration*)

pointed at both ends, light, fast, and strong. Everything needed to chase, capture, and kill a whale, even provisions to allow the men to remain away from their ship for several days if necessary, was carefully tucked inside the boats.

Every item stowed on the whaleboats had a specific function vital to the whale hunt and to the safety of the crewmen. Each small boat carried a sail, mast, and boom, and two harpoons (called "irons" by whalemen) in the bow, each five to six feet long with iron heads and wooden handles. The name of the ship, or its captain, was stamped on each in case crews from two ships pursued the same animal. Each harpoon was attached to a whale line of strong rope, tightly coiled in two containers. There were three lances (used to inflict the final death blow to the whale after the harpoon had secured it), three extra harpoons, a toggle to attach to a dead whale's carcass for towing back to the ship, a bucket

Different types of harpoons that were used by whalers to inflict the first blow on a whale *(Courtesy of the National Oceanic and Atmospheric Administration)*

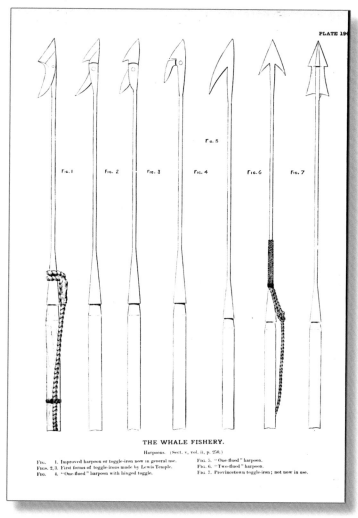

for wetting the whale line, a fog horn, matches, candles, a lantern, food, drinking water, knives, and a hatchet to cut the whale line if the whale threatened to take the boat under the water. When the *Taber* reached the Arctic, the crew would add specially designed guns to each boat's collection.

As soon as a whale was spotted, the *Taber's* crewmembers would be expected to quickly divide themselves into their assigned groups of six and climb in their boats to pursue the animal. On calm seas, in good weather, Stivers and the other ships' officers began training the crew to get in and out of the boats, row together as a team, and to perform their roles in order to successfully hunt and kill the whale.

In the training sessions the whaleboats were first lowered. Then the men, many of whom did not know how to swim, climbed into them as the smaller vessel bobbed on the waves. This was no easy task for those still trying to gain their sea

Diagram of a whaleboat *(Courtesy of the National Oceanic and Atmospheric Administration)*

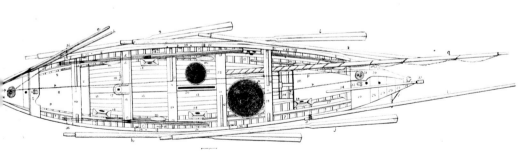

THE WHALE FISHERY.

legs. It was easy to lose one's footing and tumble into the water. Arms and legs could be crushed if an unexpected wave slammed the boat against the ship's side.

Once everyone was safely in his assigned station, the crews practiced rowing at sea. They accustomed themselves to the deep rolling sensation of small boats riding the ocean swells and learned to follow the impatient commands of the boatheaders.

Despite all the training, hunting angry, thrashing, sixty-foot whales in thirty-foot wooden boats was not something that could be taught in advance. Life and death battles with nature's largest creatures would have to be learned on-the-job.

When not training in the whaleboats or on watch duty, the *Taber's* men slept and rested below deck. Just as the ship's hierarchy determined the men's work duties and privileges, their living accommodations also reflected their rank on board.

Captain Packard had a large, private living area in the aft of the ship. The cabin where he slept was about six feet by ten feet in size and was adjacent to his own private lavatory. He also had exclusive use of another cabin that served as an office and was large enough to accommodate a sofa, table, small bookshelf, thermometer, barometer, and wood-fueled heat stove. Beyond the captain's stateroom was the aftercabin, or dining room, reserved for the exclusive use of the captain and his officers. A stairway led from there to the ship's deck.

The first, second, and third mates each had individual sleeping quarters complete with bunks and small spaces for sea chests filled with their clothes and personal items. Boatsteerers, such as Abram Briggs, were lower in rank than officers but above the regular sailors and they shared a small cabin. The ship's cooper and steward were given sleeping quarters in a tiny compartment in a section of the ship known as the steerage.

For the rest of the crew, living quarters were much more severe. At least twenty men were crowded into the narrow forecastle near the ship's bow, as far away from the ship's officers as the length of the vessel allowed. Their bunks were double stacked along the insides of the ship's walls, and the ceiling of the forecastle sat so low most men could not stand upright. The only natural light and fresh air came from a tiny hatch that was also the only way in or out. The hatch stayed closed in bad weather. Rats, cockroaches, and fleas burrowed into the food and hid on sleeping bunks and crawled on the men. On several occasions during the *Taber's* voyage, Captain Packard had to order all of the ship's openings sealed in order to exterminate the growing population of rodents with smoke.

A sailor described the forecastle as "black and slimy with filth, very small, and as hot as an oven. It was filled with a compound of foul air, smoke, sea-chests, soap-kegs, greasy pans, tainted meat. The [seamen] were smoking, laughing, chattering, and cursing the green hands who were sick. With groans on one side, and yells, oaths, laughter, and smoke on the other, it . . . did not impress . . . myself as a very pleasant home for the next year or two."

Even the timing and quality of meals were based on rank. The captain and mates ate in the aftercabin just off the captain's private quarters and sat in order of status on the ship. Ordinary sailors ate on deck when weather permitted; they ate inside the forecastle when it did not.

The *Taber*, like other nineteenth-century whaleships, did not serve high-quality food. Five weeks after departing New Bedford, Captain Packard wrote: "We are living pretty well in the cabin having fried eggs, sweet potatoes and pumpkin pies, but this will not last long."

When in port, the *Taber* was loaded with fresh fruits, vegetables, live chickens, and pigs. It was also supplied with flour, molasses, sugar, beans, butter, coffee, rice, vinegar, and barley. Stops were made at various islands along the route to the Pacific to restock food supplies with potatoes, hogs, bananas, oranges, watermelons, and coconuts. Occasionally, the men caught and ate fish and porpoise.

Throughout most of the lengthy voyage, the crew's diet was limited to meat, bread, and butter, stored for months in the ship's hold. By the time the food was dug out and served,

Rations for whaleship crew members were often poor and consisted mostly of hard bread, salt meat, and brackish water. (*Courtesy of The New Bedford Whaling Museum*)

it was usually moldy or rancid. Potatoes were often wormy and rotted. Water, kept in casks, became brackish and gave off a strong soured odor. The best of the poor provisions, of course, were served to the ship's captain and mates.

For breakfast the officers were usually served salt beef or salt pork, bread, coffee, sugar, butter, and sometimes potato hash. Boatsteerers ate the same foods but were given molasses instead of sugar and did not receive butter. Regular seamen ate salt beef or salt pork, hard bread, coffee, and molasses. Dinner was the lightest of the three meals, and all the men ate hard bread and salt pork or salt beef. Supper consisted of salt meat, bread, butter, sugar, tea, and sometimes pie or hash for the officers. Salt meat, hard tack, and tea or coffee were provided to those in the forecastle.

Three months into the voyage, Abram Briggs complained about the difference in food quality and rations given to the non-officers.

> The captain is getting so mean. He has given orders to the steward to make a barrel of flour last 20 days and two barrels of meat to last 12 days. That makes twice he, or the steward, has cut us down on the flour. The next time they cut us down we won't get any. Our gingerbread and pies we used to get twice a week each is stopped entirely. They are not going short in the cabin [where the officers were served]. Far from it. They will get enough. Tis the poor sailor that has to do all the work, [but] will have to come short.

Lack of fresh foods and dependence on salty diets for months at a time caused many seamen to suffer from vitamin deficiencies. Several of the *Taber's* crew contracted scurvy during the later months of the voyage due to their limited access to vitamin C. Scurvy usually appeared as swelling

Whaleships were required by law to carry a medicine chest onboard.
(*Courtesy of The New Bedford Whaling Museum*)

and discoloration in the legs. As the illness progressed, a man bruised easily, his gums became spongy, and his teeth loosened. As he became weaker, red sores appeared all over his body. Large doses of vitamin C found in fruits usually cured the malady. But when fresh fruits were not available, scurvy could be deadly.

American whaleships did not carry doctors. While the ships traveled to the most remote reaches of the globe, illnesses and injuries had to be treated by the ship's commander. Captain Packard served as doctor, surgeon, and dentist to his crew and found many opportunities to test his medical skills during the *Taber's* voyage. Without formal medical training, he could rely only on his own judgment and common sense when setting broken bones, amputating a sailor's arm or leg, or pulling teeth.

Accidents were common on whalers, and much of the captain's time as physician was given to repairing injuries. Loose objects occasionally fell from aloft and casks often broke free on deck or rolled dangerously around in a ship's hold during severe weather. Men could be cut while using sharp tools, burned by boiling whale blubber, or injured hauling wood. Storms and high winds occasionally caused men to fall a hundred feet from masts onto ships' decks or to be swept overboard.

The law required whaleships to carry a medicine chest, usually a wooden box about three feet high by two feet wide and two feet deep. Medicines were typically stored in glass bottles. Measuring spoons, and a device for weighing portions, were included, along with an instruction booklet. The law, however, did not specify the quantity or quality of medicines to be stored. Supplies on most whaleships were often inadequate or inappropriate for the medical needs encountered in a multiyear voyage.

It was not until December 21, two full months after the *Taber* departed from New Bedford, that first mate Stivers was able to report in his log: "Today all hands are able to do duty which is remarkable to record from the fact that from one to five hands have been off duty sick all the time since we left home. Three have been laid away with ruptures. Others from 'gripes' 'headache' 'colic' 'liver complaint.' In fact all the diseases that mankind are subject to."

four

Life at Sea

E ven while seasickness and other ailments plagued the *Taber's* crew, the ship proved to be a dependable home for the men as they journeyed across the high seas. Captain Packard wrote, "We find that our little bark can sail with the best of them." Thunderstorms soon confirmed the captain's faith in his vessel. Gale-force winds and driving rains battered the *Taber* six weeks after its New Bedford departure as it neared the equator. The ship was repeatedly forced high on the crests of huge waves and then plunged violently down into the raging water, and the crew was tumbled back and forth by the strong wind and violent waves.

"I sprang up on the weather bulwark and commenced the terrible ascent," a seaman remembered of his first experience with a storm on a similar sea voyage.

The darkness was so dense that I could scarcely see the ratlines, and it was only by groping my way in the wake of those before me, that I could at all make out where I was going. By desperate exertion, however, I succeeded, and holding on to every rope I could get hold of with extraordinary tenacity, I at length found myself on the foot-rope, leaning over the yard, and clinging to one of the reef-points, full determined not to part company with that . . . the barque was keeled over at an angle of forty-five degrees, plunging madly through the foam, and I could form no idea of the bearings of the deck. All I could see was a long dark object below, half hidden in the raging brine.

Though storms often tested the *Taber* and its crew, and daily chores filled up the long days when wind and whales were absent, the demands of sailing did not fill all the men's hours at sea. Many days on board ship, slowly sailing across the world's oceans, were routine, even boring. "Nothing in sight but a few birds," Stivers noted in his logbook mid-January.

Whaleships were often challenged by storms and squalls that threatened to sink the ship and drown the crew. *(Library of Congress)*

A SQUALL OFF CAPE HORN.

Surrounded by endless miles of water in every direction, the whalemen soon felt separated from the rest of the world. They knew, of course, that leaders in the United States were struggling to reconstruct the country's political, social, and economic foundations following the Civil War. They were aware of the election of General Ulysses S. Grant to the presidency. But most current events on land were irrelevant to the seemingly timeless existence on the *Henry Taber*.

"For the most part, a sublime uneventfulness invests you," Melville explained. "You hear no news; read no gazettes; extras with startling accounts of common places never delude you into unnecessary excitements; are never troubled with the thoughts of what you shall have for dinner—for all your

Whalemen were isolated from the rest of the world by endless miles of water, and many days at sea were uneventful and boring. *(Library of Congress)*

An illustration of two whaleship crews participating in a "gam."
(*Reproduced with the permission of the copyright owner, Imperial Tobacco, UK*)

meals for three years, or more, are snugly stowed in casks, and your bill of fare is immutable."

When the weather was good and shipboard work completed, many of the *Taber's* men assembled on deck to listen as someone played an instrument, to sing and dance, or to take turns telling stories. Captain Packard often used his leisure time to write poems about love and loneliness; Abram Briggs analyzed passages from the Bible. Many read old newspapers and well-worn books or drew pictures of scenes they saw while visiting exotic islands.

A few practiced an art typically unique to whalemen called scrimshaw. Using sailmakers' needles or other sharp-ended objects, the men carved elaborate pictures of ships,

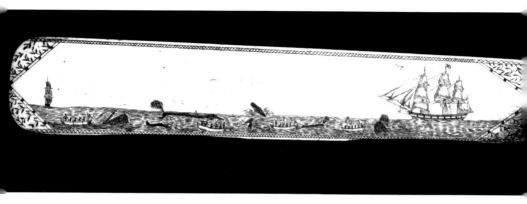

An example of scrimshaw, the art of carving pictures into whalebone or walrus tusks. *(Courtesy of The New Bedford Whaling Museum)*

whaling scenes, and images of home into walrus tusks or whale teeth. They also carved designs into homemade canes, knife handles, pie-crimpers, and dominoes. Their decorated pieces were saved to give to loved ones back home upon the ship's return.

Letters provided another form of entertainment for those who could read and write. Lonely men wrote long, loving pages to wives and lovers, mothers and children waiting for them back in New England. Whenever the *Taber* encountered a homebound vessel or docked at various ports in the Atlantic and Pacific Oceans, its crewmembers left behind mail, in the hope their letters would someday be picked up by a vessel headed to New Bedford.

Family members wrote back. Ships departing New England always had packages and notes for mariner husbands, sons, and fathers sailing on faraway seas. The longing for news from home was so deep that when the *Taber* docked in Honolulu, thirteen months after its New Bedford departure, the first thing the crew did was send someone to get their mail. Briggs diligently kept track of all nineteen letters he received during the *Taber's* voyage.

The whalemen's mail system was unreliable, of course. One wife reportedly sent more than a hundred letters to her sea captain husband over three years. He received six. When news did arrive, it was often several months old. Many men learned of the sickness of a child or the death of a loved one long after the event occurred.

The favorite pastime for the crew of the *Taber*, however, seemed to be what sailors referred to as a "gam." When two vessels spotted each other, the ships' captains would often order their ships to sail close to each other. Then, one commander and a few crewmembers would row a whaleboat to the other whaleship, while men from the second ship joined those on the first. If the captain had his wife on board, she was lowered from the ship to a whaleboat in a gamming chair to be taken on her visit. The two crews exchanged news, gossip, and books. During its three-year voyage, the *Taber's* men gammed more than fifty times with other ships.

The long days and nights crammed into a too-tight living space took a toll on men's tempers. Fights broke out on the whaleship despite threats of harsh punishment. Instances of brawling, insubordination, slowness in performing duties, attacking and insulting an officer, theft, and desertion were jotted down in the first mate's log.

According to Stivers, just as the ship was making its first of three trips into the Arctic, the cooper, Heinrick Benecke, became insolent and refused to do his duties. When confronted, he struck Stivers. A fistfight ensued that Benecke lost. He was "sent to the masthead at 4:00 p.m. [and] called down at 9 p.m." The next morning, Benecke came from below deck and attempted to escape by jumping overboard into the icy ocean water. A few crewmembers threw a small raft to him, lowered a boat, and rowed out to pick him up. Once Benecke was back on board the ship, Stivers kicked and punched him. According to Stivers, Benecke then pleaded with Captain Packard to put him ashore. The captain gave the man his trunk and let him go.

"Called all hands at 3 o'clock this morning and took our anchor for the Arctic to cruise, leaving our cooper on shore," wrote Captain Packard. It was the captain's only reference to the entire incident.

Desertions were common on whaleships, and the *Taber* was no exception. Many men who initially signed did not fully understand the dirty, difficult life they had chosen. Others could not tolerate the rigid rules and structure of ship life. After months of grueling work, isolation at sea, and lack of control over their lives, some sailors chose to sneak away from the ship when it finally anchored at a port. Punishment was severe for those caught and returned.

Desertion was difficult to manage. Ships sailed with just enough men to accomplish their necessary tasks, and the loss of a single man increased the work loads for those remaining behind. Each whaleboat required six men, and losing one—especially a boatsteerer—could mean one less boat available for chasing whales.

On March 8, 1869, three men attempted to desert the *Taber* after it anchored in New Zealand. They were captured the following day by island natives and returned to the ship. Briggs made note of the event in his journal and added his own opinion: "caught the three men that we thought had run away. I think it is all false. They had no intention of running away." There was no formal investigation and no trial. The captain ordered them put "in irons" and confined below deck.

The use of crude iron handcuffs was the favored punishment. Depending on the severity of misdemeanors, a man's hands would be cuffed in front of his body or with his wrists locked behind his back. Sometimes, both his hands and feet were restrained. The man would endure the punishment confined on deck, below in a cabin, or in the ship's "run."

The "run" was a small hole under the deck, too small to allow a man to stand. There was no light, and the only air carried the suffocating stench of bilge-water. Imprisonment in the run could last for several days, or even weeks. Briggs noted that the three men were released the following day to help load provisions on board the ship, but were returned to irons at sundown.

Although no instances of flogging were noted in the 1868-71 logbooks and journals of the *Henry Taber*, the practice had been common on whaleships in the first half of the nineteenth century. When a man disobeyed a ship's officer or ship policy, he risked being stripped of his clothes down to his waist. Then his wrists were tied together and lashed over his head to the rigging so that his feet barely touched the deck. One of the ship's officers would slash the man's back repeatedly with a heavy rope. When the punishment ended the flesh on the man's back was in shreds and bleeding and he was cut down and sent below to have his wounds treated. It was a brutal, cruel way to enforce the authority of the captain on a whaler, and many men died from the extent of the lashings or the infections that sometimes formed on their wounds. The

The American consulate in Honolulu provided aid to American sailors and arbitrated any disputes between captain and crew. *(Library of Congress)*

United States outlawed whipping seamen for punishment in 1850, but the law was not always enforced.

Sailors who believed they were unjustly punished or that their punishments were too harsh did have some recourse when the ship docked at a major harbor. When the *Taber* anchored in Honolulu in November 1869, all of the men who had been punished for fighting, insubordination, and attempted desertion went to the office of the American consul with their grievances against Captain Packard and his officers.

Hawaii, then known as the Sandwich Islands, was not yet part of the United States. The consulate on Hawaii's island of Oahu represented the American government. Among his primary duties, the consulate lent aid to American sailors who were sick, stranded, or had been mistreated while working on U.S. ships in the Pacific Ocean.

"I can not see it," wrote Captain Packard in his journal about the sailors' complaints. "They have been used as well as any crew I ever was with, always having enough to eat."

The captain believed the men were trying to get out of completing their five-year contracts. A deserter forfeited all rights to any monies already earned, but a man who could convince the consul he had been mistreated would be released from all obligation to the ship and receive his pay for work done. He could leave the ship to work on another or to set up house on one of the tropical islands of the South Pacific. The American consul in Honolulu, Thomas Adamson, listened to the angry crewmembers but determined they did not have a case. The consul told the men to go back to work.

The consulate did not brush aside Captain Packard's decisions regarding Heinrich Benecke, however. Benecke was the man Stivers had beaten for attempted desertion and whom Captain Packard had put ashore while the ship was making its first journey to the Arctic in the spring of 1869. The consulate filed a certificate to prosecute the captain for violation of the laws of the United States for discharging Benecke so far away from its jurisdiction. "The fact that the seaman consented to being put ashore," wrote Consul Adamson in a letter to the U.S. Secretary of State in Washington D.C., "does not, in my opinion, mitigate the offense, for the beating he had received from the officer of the vessel no doubt made him willing to accept any alternative rather than remain on the vessel." Apparently, no action was taken against the captain and the *Taber* soon resumed its multiyear voyage.

Except for the fact that the *Henry Taber* was at sea for more than half a year before the crew sighted a single whale, daily life during the first part of the voyage was typical. Work, boredom, friendships, fights, rebellions, and punishments—all were similar to most American whaleships in the years following the American Civil War. But Abram Briggs' logbook entry on April 8, 1869, seemed to foreshadow the future: "Something tells me in my own mind that we will not make our fortunes this voyage . . . ."

five

The Floating Factory

There blooooooows!

This was the shout every whaleman hoped to hear. A lookout, stationed on the mast high above the deck of a whaleship, would yell these words as soon as he spotted the spray of a distant whale blowing into the air.

The crew of the *Henry Taber* first heard the shout as their ship sailed across the Bering Sea towards the hunting waters of the Arctic. The crew rushed to the ship's sides and lowered their whaleboats onto the water. The pursuit of their first great whale had begun.

The *Taber* had been sailing for almost eight months without capturing a single whale. As weeks and months passed, the frustrated crew grew increasingly restless. Lack of whales meant there would be little or no pay for the crew. Stivers ended most of his journal entries with the disappointed words "Nothing in sight." Capturing this first whale was important, not only for economic reasons, but for the crew's morale.

Captain Packard and his officers each assumed control of the whaleboats as "boatheaders." With an eager crew of six men in each vessel, they swiftly steered the boats to the whale's last known position.

Shipkeeper David Edwards remained on board the *Taber* to manage the ship in the captain's absence. He also monitored the movements of the whale from the ship's mast since the boats rode low in the water and could easily lose sight of it. Using agreed upon signals, Edwards kept the whaleboat crews apprised of the whale's location and let them know each time it swam near the surface or dove deep into the water.

The whaleboat crews maneuvered to the area where they believed the whale would surface. First mate John Stivers's boat arrived before the others. As boatsteerer, Abram Briggs was responsible for driving the first harpoon into the animal. Briggs carefully rose and stood still in the bow, his harpoon poised for the strike.

As boatheader, Stivers faced Briggs from his position at the boat's stern as he silently scanned the deep ocean waters. The bowman, midship oarsman, tub oarsman, and after oarsman all sat motionless and quiet, facing away from Briggs. As soon as Briggs threw his harpoon, the oarsmen would quickly row the wooden boat away from the angry animal's thrashing flukes and biting jaws.

There was a chance the whale had left the area and would surface miles away, out of sight of the boat and even shipkeeper Edward's line of vision. But if the animal was feeding in the deep waters below the men's position, it would soon return to the top.

The whale finally surfaced less than half a mile away, violently expelling air and water from its blowhole. The boat

A boatsteerer poised to strike the first blow with his harpoon *(Courtesy of The New Bedford Whaling Museum)*

thrust into motion and Briggs steadied himself as the crew vigorously pulled at their oars to get the boat within attack range. Once they were close to the whale, oars were stowed away in favor of paddles, which were quieter. The men spoke only in whispers as Stivers maneuvered the boat out of the whale's line of vision. Briggs resumed his silent position at the bow of the boat once more, raised his six-foot long harpoon iron, with its sharp toggle at the end, and pressed his knee against the boat's bow for balance. At the precise moment boat and beast aligned, Stivers jerked the boat to the whale's side and shouted for Briggs to pitch his weapon into the whale's flesh. Briggs' iron hit its mark.

The men thrust their oars deep into the water and furiously tried to back the boat away from the angry, hurt, sixty-foot-long, one hundred-ton whale. Every man on board knew a thrashing whale could snap the small wooden boat into pieces.

The whale raised its flukes and slammed angrily against the sea, nearly slashing the boat in half. Briggs switched positions with Stivers, as tradition dictated. It would be Stivers's honor, as boatheader, to use his lance to inflict the final death-blow when the opportunity allowed.

The whale took off at an incredible speed, its fleeing body still attached to the boat by the strong rope. The whale's high-speed dash dragged the bouncing vessel behind it, over the ocean swells, in what whalers called a Nantucket sleigh ride. The men, quickly drenched in sea spray, struggled to keep their arms and legs from getting tangled in whale line.

The tub oarsman frantically poured water over the stretched rope to prevent friction sparks. He kept an axe nearby to cut the rope if the whale decided to dive deep, taking the boat down with it.

Finally, when the men and their whaleboat were several miles away from the *Taber*, the whale tired and stopped. As it floated on the water, the ocean's rise and fall washing over it, Briggs steered the boat closer to the whale's side, careful to remain out of sight of its side-positioned eyes. The whale's hearing was acute: although wounded and scared, if alerted

The whaleboat in this print is being dragged behind a speeding whale. *(Courtesy of the National Oceanic and Atmospheric Administration)*

to their presence, it would likely thrash at the men or try again to swim to safety.

"I often think that if persons who use lamp oil at home," wrote a young nineteenth-century whaleman, "could but just see all that a whaleman is compelled to undergo, by way of hardship, danger, and suffering, from the time a whale is 'raised' from the mast-head, 'til he is 'stowed-down' in the hold—if they only knew at what a fearful risk of life and limb he launches forth upon the bosom of the mighty ocean in a small frail boat—if they could but see him 'hauling up' to the thundering flukes or open jaws of a whale—then, if they could but see that boat mashed to atoms and a crew of six men struggling for life in a sea of blood,—a loud and mighty voice

As depicted in this print, an angry, wounded, thrashing whale posed a very real threat to the men in the whaleboat.

would go up to those in authority praying that he might be treated as a man on his ship."

Soon the whale was too tired to battle further. As soon as Briggs realigned the boat with the weary animal, the oarsmen grabbed hold of the harpoon line and began pulling against the huge whale, forcing it closer to the surface.

Stivers lifted his long, sleek lance, with its razor-sharp blade, and took aim at the spot where the whale's arteries met near its heart and lungs. He stabbed the lance deep into the animal's body, and the whale's lungs immediately flooded with blood. The whale spouted the blood high into the air and rolled on its side.

The men waited until the giant animal stopped moving before approaching it again. Stivers poked its eye with the lance to ensure it was dead. The others cut a hole in the whale's flukes and slid a rope through to allow them to tow the beast back to their ship.

It was a gruesome killing but during the nineteenth century few considerations were given to animals' rights. Whaling was an admirable occupation.

This Currier & Ives print shows a whaleboat attacking a whale as the whaleship in the background is in the process of "cutting in" and "trying out." *(Library of Congress)*

On June 18, 1869, after eight long months at sea, Stivers and his tired boat crew towed their first whale to the *Henry Taber*. Pulling the enormous carcass through the ocean water proved difficult, but the animal had to be chained to the *Taber's* side, and its blubber removed, before sharks began feeding on it.

After a brief rest and a quick meal on board the ship, the entire crew began the grueling work of slicing and boiling the whale's blubber into gallons of oil. The processes of "cutting in" and "trying out" the whale could take hours or days, depending on the size of the animal and the skill of the crew. The *Taber* was transformed into a floating factory.

Whalers "cutting in" or stripping whale blubber. *(Courtesy of The Granger Collection)*

A cutting stage, made of three long wooden planks, was suspended over the whale. The *Taber* was maneuvered so the pressure of the wind would push the whale towards the ship's side in order to balance the vessel in the water against the additional weight. The slow process of removing layers of blubber began, a process called "cutting in."

Stivers and the other mates stepped onto the cutting stage and inserted a massive hook into the whale's side. The other end of the hook was attached to a winch, or windlass, turned by several men on deck. They peeled off a thick strip of the animal's blubber, called a blanket piece, as the whale rotated. A single blanket piece was twelve to eighteen feet long, six feet wide, and twelve to eighteen inches thick. It could weigh

THE WHALE FISHERY.

" A ship on the Northwest coast of America cutting in her last right whale." (Sect, v, vol. ii, p 277.)

Drawing by H. W. Elliott, from a French lithograph designed by B. Russell, of New Bedford.

PLATE 207

This illustration shows the massive size of a whale's jawbone and baleen plates as it is being raised aboard the ship. *(Courtesy of the National Oceanic and Atmospheric Administration)*

up to 2,000 pounds. Each piece required a dozen men to lift it onto the ship's deck.

The blanket piece was then lowered through an opening to the dark and bloody blubber room below. Several men in the blubber room worked to cut each long, heavy piece into smaller, more manageable chunks. The cut pieces resembled pages in a book and were called "Bible leaves." All remaining flesh was trimmed off before the pieces were returned to the deck for boiling. The crew worked in six-hour shifts around the clock until the job was complete.

The work was tiring and dangerous, even in the best possible weather conditions. Men could slip overboard as the deck became slick with blood and oil, or be fatally crushed by the enormous strips of blubber. Injuries from sharp cutting tools, and burns from scalding oil, were common as the ship rocked on the ocean waves. When squalls or gales blew over the *Taber*, the complexity and dangers associated with the entire process increased tremendously.

Eliza Williams, wife of Captain Thomas Williams of the bark *Monticello*, witnessed the work while she was a passenger on her husband's whaleship. Her husband's crew had captured two whales and she described the difficulty the men encountered while cutting-in and trying out the animals:

> I thought it was impossible for them to work at all with the waves dashing up against the ship and those huge [whales] moving up and down in the water, sometimes so covered that you could scarcely see them. But they worked on and did not cease. There was a complete din of noises on deck—the wind, the rain, the officers shouting to the men, the mincing machine, and altogether it was a confused place.

The *Taber's* crew dropped the chunks of blubber into large iron pots fitted over fire pits built on the main deck. Known as "tryworks," the pots served as a shipboard furnace that boiled the whale's blubber into oil.

The men constantly stirred the slow-forming liquid to prevent burning. Any discoloration to the final product would render their catch less valuable on the oil market back home. As the oil hissed in the trypots, scraps of remaining skin were skimmed off and recycled to feed the fires.

"The smell of the oil is quite offensive to me," wrote Mrs. Williams. "The constant noise of heavy chains on deck, the driving of the hoops, the turning over of the casks of oil til it seemed as if the ship shook, and the loud orders of the Officers—all together, would make a nervous person go distracted I think, but it cannot be avoided on board a whale ship."

Some of the oil was set aside to light the ship's decks at night in order for the men to continue working as darkness fell over the ocean. All night, the glow of small lanterns and large trypot fires could be seen for miles. As dawn broke, huge clouds of black smoke had formed in the sky above the ship.

"A trying-out scene has something peculiarly wild and savage in it," remembered J. Ross Browne on his whaling voyage. "There is a murderous appearance about the blood-stained decks, and the huge masses of flesh and blubber lying here and there, and a ferocity in the looks of the men, heightened by the red, fierce glare of the fires, which inspire in the mind of the novice feelings of mingled disgust and awe."

Hot oil was poured into tanks and later transferred to large casks on deck until it reached air temperature. Once cooled, the casks were taken to the ship's hold for storage. Each cask was about five feet high and four feet in diameter at the middle. Each could hold thirty-one and a half gallons of oil.

While men continued to cut-in and tryout the whale's blubber, a rope was tied around Briggs's waist (to prevent him from slipping into the sea), and he was lowered onto what remained of the whale's carcass. Since he had been the first to strike the animal during the hunt, it was Briggs's responsibility—and honor—to chop through two feet of bone mass in order to detach the whale's jaw.

Seawater swirled around Briggs's legs as he balanced on the whale's slippery body. He hacked at the whale while

This illustration shows whale by-products being used in a variety of products such as corsets, umbrellas, lamp oil, and fertilizer. *(Courtesy of Oxford Science Archive/HIP/The Image Works)*

the rolling of the ship pushed seawater as high as his neck. Hungry sharks circled nearby. As soon as Briggs managed to separate the whale's jaw from the rest of its body, the section was raised to the deck of the ship.

The waiting crew removed the baleen, referred to as "bone," from the whale's mouth. Baleen was divided in two sections, each weighing more than one thousand pounds, which the men had to cut into smaller pieces for cleaning.

White gum was scraped from the plates of baleen with knives or pieces of sharp coconut. Then the baleen was soaked

This scene shows two crew members lashing baleen into the traditional eighty-pound bundles for storage in the hold. *(Courtesy of New York Public Library)*

PACKING WHALEBONE. *HM June 1860 New Bedf*

in water for about twenty hours, washed with sand and water, and then polished until shiny. It was a time-consuming process, but if not carefully done, the baleen kept a strong fish odor and its market value decreased.

The clean whalebone was spread out on deck or in the rigging to dry. Later, the crew lashed the pieces together in eighty-pound bundles and stored them in the hold below deck. Then they scrubbed the ship's decks, and their own clothes, to remove the strong odor of smoked blubber.

Rats on the ship often gnawed the bone. If signs of damage were visible, the men moved the bone back on deck and, as soon as they were able, "smoked" the ship (to kill the rats) by setting fires below deck and sealing all cracks. The crew remained above deck for the rest of the day.

While the crewmembers of the *Taber* labored over their first whale catch, Captain Packard ordered a lookout to remain stationed high above the ship's deck, searching the sea for more whales. Depending on the size of whales caught, the captain knew he would need oil and bone from at least a dozen more whales to fill his ship's hold.

six

Troubles in the Pacific

Working in the North Pacific and Arctic Oceans throughout 1869, the crew of the *Henry Taber* captured ten large whales. In 1870, they caught seventeen. At the end of both Arctic seasons, Captain Packard ordered his ship to depart the lucrative whaling grounds in late September. He would have remained in the region throughout most of October, as other whaleships did, if the *Taber* had been larger and able to hold more oil.

"We cannot take any more," the captain lamented in his logbook, "as we have no room for them. Our ship is small and our casks are all full. . . . If we had plenty of room our chance would be good for twelve hundred [barrels] this season but we are bound off with about 850 [barrels]. It seems kind of hard but so it is."

He navigated southbound to Hawaii. The harbor at Honolulu, the largest of the islands' communities, was a stopping port for whaleships to unload their cargoes of oil and baleen onto

The harbor of Honolulu was a valuable port, utilized by whaleships to restock supplies and unload cargoes. *(Courtesy of The Granger Collection)*

merchant vessels bound for the United States. While in port, Captain Packard could also restock the *Taber's* food provisions and allow his men to enjoy much-needed time away from ship.

Anchored within sight of Honolulu's warm, white beaches and swaying palm trees, the crew of the *Henry Taber* finished washing, drying, and bundling their hard-earned whalebone. They scurried up the ship's rigging to loosen the sails and air them out. They heaved heavy casks of oil from their ship on to others bound for market. Only after the immediate demands of the *Taber* had been attended were the men allowed to go ashore several hours each day for rest and recreation.

Captain Packard took advantage of the warm weather to recover from a severe bout of rheumatism. Two weeks after the *Taber* reached Honolulu's harbor, he left the ship and went to the island of Maui to recuperate. In the captain's absence, first mate Stivers supervised the *Taber* and ensured supplies were delivered and properly stowed in anticipation of the ship's return to the Arctic. Fresh water, potatoes, coconuts, yams, bananas, and wood were packed in the ship's hold. Chickens and pigs were penned on its deck.

During the captain's absence, a man deserted from the *Taber* and several more were discharged due to illness. Stivers hired eighteen "Kanakas" (a Hawaiian word meaning "people" or "men") to fill the *Taber's* diminished ship roster. The native Hawaiians had reputations for being strong, reliable seamen.

Abram Briggs was promoted to fourth mate and given command of his own whaleboat as boatheader instead of boatsteerer. On January 1, 1871, Briggs wrote in his personal journal, "A Happy New Year to all," and then scribbled in the narrow margin at the bottom of the page, "and good luck attend me this year with thanks."

Recovered from his illness, Captain Packard returned to the ship on January 14, 1871, and resumed his command. With a lookout posted high above the ship's deck scanning the seas for signs of whales, the captain navigated the *Taber* away from the tranquil Sandwich Islands once more. He planned to search for sperm whales in the South Pacific until spring and then turn northward for another challenging bowhead whale hunting season in the Arctic.

Tropical temperatures and easy sailing, however, did not bring luck to the *Taber's* crew. Briggs damaged his ankle while trying to move a heavy cask of bread. The ship's carpenter became extremely ill and could not perform his duties. There was a fistfight between a sailor and Stivers, several

Map of Bering Sea, showing the latitude and longitude zones of the Universal Transverse Mercator coordinate system, from 56U to 10W. As the *Henry Taber* moved north across the latitude degrees, the weather turned colder, and the men quit fighting and started cooperating.

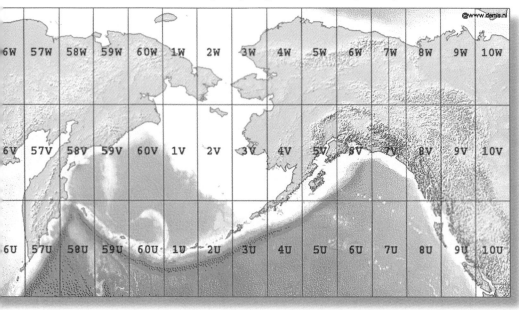

attempts at desertion, and at one point, the cabin boy was sent "to the forecastle for thieving and being untrustworthy and for being good for nothing generally in the capacity as cabin boy."

Regardless of the troubles on board, or perhaps due to the possibility of more attempted desertions if the ship dropped anchor near a comfortable port, Captain Packard steered the *Taber* in a wide arc around Hawaii when the time came to turn northbound.

Temperatures cooled with each degree of latitude crossed and so did the men's tempers. Nearing the frigid waters of the Bering Sea, the men set aside their fighting and discontentment in order to focus on the difficult tasks ahead. They had learned from past experiences that cooperation offered their only chance for successful hunting in Arctic waters. In 1871, they would discover that their lives also depended upon it.

seven
Gathering of the Arctic Fleet

I n the nineteenth century, the entire area north of the Bering Strait was known to whalers simply as the "Arctic" and encompassed the Chukchi Sea, Beaufort Sea, Amundsen Gulf, and the eastern waters of the East Siberian Sea. Since the first American whaleship, named *Superior*, had sailed north of the Bering Strait in 1848 and discovered a large number of bowhead whales, hundreds of ships had sojourned into the far northern reaches of the globe.

The Arctic was notorious for difficult weather patterns and ship-crushing ice. Fierce blowing winds frequently rushed down from the northwest, delivering heavy snows. Strong currents were known to push massive floes of ice across water faster than wind-dependent whaleships could flee to safety. Every seasoned sailor had heard stories of men and ships lost to the region's treacherous conditions.

Arctic waters could be treacherous. *(Library of Congress)*

The most recent tale told on ships' decks involved the British whaleship *Japan*. The vessel had sailed into the Arctic in the summer of 1870 but did not sail out.

It was believed the *Japan* had been destroyed during a heavy storm. The captain, Frederick Barker, and his crew were assumed dead. Whalemen speculated that even if a storm had not drowned the *Japan's* sailors, the nine-month-long Arctic winter had killed them through starvation or exposure.

Yet in spite of the harrowing stories and well-known dangers, Arctic whaling had become vital to the oil and baleen markets of the world and to the whalemen who ventured there. So much was to be gained that sea captains studied the region's weather to find patterns that would allow them to remain longer each year. Most felt confident whaling from June until late September or early October. After that, the captains knew winter winds would blow across the Arctic

Sea ice *(Courtesy of the National Oceanic and Atmospheric Administration)*

waters and force miles of floating ice towards shore. The key to success was to leave just before winter arrived.

The *Henry Taber* reached the edge of the Arctic pack ice on May 7, 1871. For several weeks, the ship was only able to cruise along the ice's edge, waiting for warmer temperatures and winds to break the ice up enough to allow the ship to continue on its northerly quest.

With no whales in sight and his ship's duties accomplished, the recently promoted Abram Briggs had time to track the arrival of other whaling vessels in his journal. Many of their names reflected people and places important to the American whaling industry: *Oliver Crocker, Oriole, Concordia, Elizabeth Swift, Contest, George Howland, John Wells, Massachusetts, Fanny, Monticello, Gay Head,* and the *Thomas Dickason.*

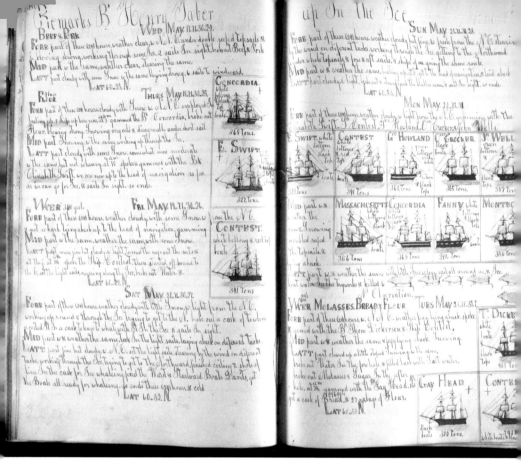

These pages from the logbook of Abram Briggs, written while waiting for the arctic ice to melt, document the arrival of other whaling vessels. (*Courtesy of The New Bedford Whaling Museum*)

Unlike Captain Packard of the *Henry Taber*, the commanders of the *Monticello*, *Fanny*, and *Emily Morgan* had brought their wives and children with them. This was common practice because of the length of most whaling voyages. It is estimated that one-sixth of all whaling captains took their families to sea.

Wives and children ate the same poor-quality, limited-variety food as the crew, suffered from many of the same life-threatening illnesses, and endured raging storms and rolling seas. They battled endless months and years of loneliness, isolation, and boredom. Yet, for most, life at sea was an acceptable alternative to the long separations the whaling industry imposed on families.

Wives were not assigned any official duties on whaling ships. Jobs often considered "women's work" on land, such as cooking, cleaning, and mending, were done exclusively by men. Most captains' wives quietly passed their sea lives sewing, mending, and cleaning their own family's few articles of clothing. They wrote letters, kept diaries, and read everything they could. They also gave birth and raised their children. Occasionally, a captain would permit his wife to nurse sick crewmembers or to learn navigation as a hobby. But for the most part, a woman's only responsibility was to stay out of the crew's way while the men went about the ship's duties, especially when a whale was caught.

For a captain's children, voyages had both positive and negative consequences. Instead of being away from their father for years at a time, they got to be with him and to see him work. They were able to travel around the world and be exposed to different languages and customs. They tasted strange foods, saw exotic animals, and spent time with their parents that few children had the opportunity to enjoy.

Yet, young boys and girls passed months of their lives confined in the limited space of a whaleship with little exercise or fresh foods. When the ship encountered violent weather, children spent days below deck in the cramped captain's quarters unable to come above for fresh air.

Even good weather conditions offered children few opportunities for entertainment at sea, and even less room to run and play. One mother wrote:

> The system of watches meant that at all times, except at meal times and in the early evening dogwatch, some one of the officers would be sleeping in his room at the forward end of the afterhouse . . . noisy romping by the children [was] taboo except for those evening hours. The children played quietly on the starboard side of the deck if it was the mate's watch below and to port if it was the second mate's. On our ship, we became quite ingenious in developing quiet games.

Mothers did their best to provide some academic education. Math and reading skills were addressed most days. When a whale was caught, the lessons were suspended so the children could watch the men work.

It was a difficult way to raise a family, and many captains' wives, and their children, would travel for only a portion of a voyage and then set up temporary homes in foreign ports when the ships stopped to refuel and resupply. The largest number of whaling families settled in the Sandwich Islands, especially in the communities of Honolulu, Lahaina, and Hilo. A few months on land, in the tropical climate of the South Pacific, was a welcome change from tedious months at sea. It was also a safe alternative to braving the dangerous waters of the Arctic.

Captain Packard did not bring his family. The three-year voyage of the *Henry Taber* was the longest stretch of time he had been absent from home since his two children were born. He missed them and devoted dozens of poems and songs to them in the pages of his logbook. In one called "Little Mary's Song," he tells of a daughter begging her seafaring father to return home and comfort her after her brother's death. Captain Packard's son did not die while he was at sea, but at one point on his voyage he had a nightmare that the tragic event had actually occurred.

Father, dear Father, come home with me now,
The clock in the steeple strikes three!
The house is so lonely, the hours so long,
For poor weeping Mother and me.
Yes, we are alone, poor Benny is dead,
And gone with the angels of light!
And these were the very last words that he said,
I want to kiss papa good night!
Come home, come home, come home,
Please Father, dear Father, come home.

Fourth mate Abram Briggs continued to track the arrival of other whaleships at the edge of the Arctic pack ice and also sketched detailed pictures of the vessels in the pages of his journal. He drew each vessel's masts and sails inside neat square borders, paying careful attention to any defining features before writing the ships' names above. He kept track of the gamming taking place between the gathered ships. He

Briggs documented the arrival of other whaling vessels similar to these in the Arctic. *(Courtesy of Library of Congress)*

quizzed himself on stories from his Bible and complained about the unbearably cold temperatures.

Eventually forty ships gathered at the boundary between ice and sea. More than 1,400 crewmembers eagerly studied the frozen barrier for signs of movement that would allow them to proceed north. Twenty-one of the ships in attendance were from New Bedford. The assembly of so many ships from a similar home port, some owned by the same investors, became a reunion for many ships' sailors, women, and children. All had been away from home for several months— most for several years. When weather permitted, they rowed

This painting shows a desperate crew trying to salvage cargo and supplies from a ship that is trapped in ice. *(Courtesy of the Bridgeman Art Library)*

from ship to ship in whaleboats to visit and exchange food, books, sewing materials, and information.

Camaraderie among whaling crews was not simply a reaction to the lonely lives of sailors at sea. Temporary unity could prove vital to the safety of men and cargoes traveling the hazardous Arctic waters. Over the years, many sailors had been taken aboard competing ships when their own were destroyed by hidden reefs or stove by fast-moving ice. Food and tools were often traded among the different crews. If a whaleboat became separated from its home-vessel due to darkness, fog, or distance, shelter was gladly provided to its

The Arctic region

![The Arctic region map]

sailors by another ship. As always in the Arctic, strength was found in numbers when ice caused a ship to go aground.

A tradition had developed ensuring that ships trapped in ice, and those forced ashore trying to avoid it, could depend on men from other vessels to lend aid. As a team, cooperating crews might try to ram the ship through the ice, or set up a system of winches to free it. If there was open water nearby, they could tie whaleboats to the vessel and attempt to pull it to safety. Industrious captains had been known to fill bottles with gun powder, tie them to long poles, shove them under the ice and blast their ships clear. One whaleship captain explained that "Arctic ice isn't like any other kind. It is never smooth, for example. When it starts to make, little cakes form, the size of a plate. They mass together and keep getting larger and larger, then it piles into points and ridges. At times there is no ice in sight, and then suddenly it will appear and pile up terribly." Collaboration among the crews was often the difference between an inconvenience and a disaster.

eight
Early Warning

In June, the spring ice began to break up and the loosely organized western Arctic whaling fleet of 1871 began a slow advance north-northeast along the Alaskan coastline. Captain Packard kept lookouts aloft in the crow's nest of the *Taber* to spot open channels in the ice through which the ships could travel. The lookout shouted to the officer on deck when a change of course was necessary. The officer then ordered the helmsman to steer the ship in an appropriate direction. When ice floes opened, the ship followed the cracks; when the ice closed, the *Taber* stopped and waited. It was slow going as the ship zigzagged back and forth through the ice.

As the *Taber* and other vessels were rounding St. Lawrence Island in the Bering Sea on June 5, lookouts on the *John Wells* spotted a surprising sight coming from shore. A canoe was being rowed rapidly toward the whaleships, the men on board waving frantically for attention. From a distance,

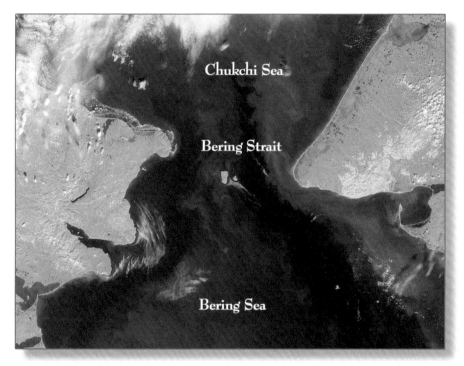

The crew of the *Henry Taber* were among those who rescued the survivors of the whaling ship *Japan* in the Bering Sea. *(Courtesy of NASA)*

the approaching men looked like Chukchi natives eager to trade with the first whalers to arrive in the region that season. But as the canoe came closer, it became clear the men were not Arctic natives. They were the British survivors of the whaleship *Japan*, shipwrecked in a terrible storm the year before.

The *John Wells* and *Henry Taber*, along with several other whaleships, quickly maneuvered to rescue their shipwrecked comrades. Crew members of the *Taber* assisted Captain Frederick Barker, commander of the doomed *Japan*, onto their ship's deck. The disheveled captain told of his vessel's violent destruction and the resulting hardships he and his

Captain Frederick Barker *(Courtesy of The New Bedford Whaling Museum)*

men had endured during the Arctic's brutal winter months. Details of his ordeal held the complete attention of the *Taber's* officers and crew.

"The gale blew harder," Captain Barker remembered of the *Japan's* misfortune, "attended by such a terrible blinding snow that we could not see half a ship's length. The ship had been running under lower topsails and storm sails, but owning to the strength of the gale, was making racehorse speed. The helm was put starboard and braced up sharp, when . . . just then, to add to our horrors, a huge wave swept over the ship, taking off all the boats and sweeping the decks clean . . . death truly stared us in the face."

He described another wave, more violent than the first that swallowed the *Japan* in one enormous swoop and then mercilessly flung what remained of the ship against the rocky shallows. The *Japan* was completely destroyed. Thirty of Captain Barker's men managed to swim or crawl to shore. Chukchis natives living nearby rushed to their aid.

The *Taber's* men listened as the British captain told of being lifted onto a stretcher by the Chukchi and then carried across the beach towards their village. He recalled being taken past dead bodies of frozen sailors scattered along the shore. "The air was piercing cold and several of my men, being unable to dry their clothes, had fallen by the wayside and died. I found that out of a crew of thirty stout, stalwart sailors, eight men had frozen to death."

The Chukchis cared for Captain Barker and his surviving crewmembers to the extent their limited resources of food, clothing, and shelter allowed. Temperatures during the winter dropped to fifty degrees below zero, Fahrenheit. In the journal Captain Barker kept during the long winter, he wrote how the circumstances "rendered me nearly desperate enough to take my life."

It was a sad tale, told many times in the days after the rescue. "Let us hope," wrote Abram Briggs on June 20, 1871, "[the] all wise being will permit the rescued ones to return to their friends, no more to partake of the trials and troubles of the Arctic Ocean."

But the misfortunes of the *Japan's* crew did not end with their June rescue. Stivers noted in his log that the *Japan's* shipwrecked crewmen were "all laid up with sores broke out all over their bodies, feet and hands." None of the fleet's whaleships could afford to abandon the potential profits promised by the lucrative Arctic whaling season in order to transport the *Japan's* survivors to hospitals in Honolulu or San Francisco. The shipwrecked sailors had to remain with the fleet as it worked in the region for the next five months. Those that were physically able were expected to help with ship duties in return for their food and shelter.

As the fleet prepared to resume its northbound heading, Chukchis who had cared for the *Japan's* men visited the ships to warn the arriving captains that a bad winter season was predicted for 1871. The natives believed massive amounts of ice and fierce winds would return earlier than usual that year, endangering the fleet's normal exit routes out of the Arctic. They encouraged the whalers to abandon the year's hunt and head south once more.

But the commanders had confidence in their own knowledge and experience of the Arctic's weather patterns. Most had sailed the waters many times in past years and felt well trained in its environmental hazards. It was possible, they knew, for a ship to be caught in an unexpected storm, stove by ice, or grounded on shore. Still, believing they possessed a great amount of skill and a fair amount of luck, the captains were determined to whale in the Arctic until early October.

The Arctic whaling season was too important to the financial stability of the whaling industry to justify turning the ships around and heading away because a few natives thought the weather was going to be difficult. The ships'

Despite the dangerous, ship-sinking ice, the whaleship fleet of 1871 continued to move north into the Arctic whaling grounds. *(Courtesy of The Bridgeman Art Library)*

owners would never accept that line of reasoning, nor would the fleet's 1,400 seamen, who were eager to earn their livings hunting bowhead whales. The commanders ignored the dire forecast of the natives and ordered their ships to continue north as planned.

The natives' predictions had more of a scientific basis than the whalers realized. Unknown to seafarers in the 1800s, several times each century atmospheric conditions caused a stationary high pressure system to develop off northeastern Siberia. The change in weather pattern caused cold onshore winds to significantly delay springtime ice decay. The whalers frequently noted the lingering ice in their logbooks and journals in 1871, but no one had any idea of what was happening meteorologically.

Frustrated with their inability to quickly get the ships north to areas where whales were believed to have migrated, the captains ordered their crews to temporarily hunt walruses instead. A mature walrus yielded up to three-quarters of a barrel of oil and could bring as much profit as regular whale oil. Because walrus tusks also brought some income, hunting the animals helped fill the whaleships' holds in the absence of whale sightings.

Natives of the Arctic regions had long depended on the walrus population for their survival. They needed the animals' meat and blubber for food, the skin to construct boats and houses, and tusks to make tools. The whalers, with their guns and profit motives, had severely depleted the walrus population over the years and damaged the Arctic's balance between man and nature.

The resulting suffering of native populations who depended upon walruses was so great that Captain Barker, of the *Japan*, later took up the cause to end the practice. He wrote to a New Bedford newspaper about his shipwrecked time in the Arctic and how he had survived the brutal winter thanks to the generosity of natives and their limited supply of walrus meat: "Should I ever come to the Arctic Ocean to cruise

The native tribes of the Arctic region have traditionally used walrus meat for food, walrus skin for shelter, and walrus tusks for tools. *(Library of Congress)*

again, I will never catch another walrus, for these poor people along the coast have nothing else to live upon. . . . I felt like a guilty culprit while eating their food with them, that I have been taking bread out of their mouths, yet although they knew that the whaleships are doing this, they still were ready to share all they had with us."

The tools and techniques for successful walrus hunting required the crew of the *Taber* to temporarily remove their whaling equipment from their boats and to replace it with special knives and gear. A walrus boat carried only a mate, two crewmembers, two guns and ammunition. Because walruses have an excellent sense of smell, boats were maneuvered downwind from where the animals congregated on the shore. About a half-mile away from a large, sleepy herd, a boat would be slowed and the men inside it would quietly begin rowing toward their prey. It could take several hours to reach the pack at the measured pace.

Once close enough to ensure a hit, the mate aimed his gun at one of the sleeping animals. Success demanded patience and good aim. If a walrus was shot in such a way that it fell into the water, all the other walruses would dive in. The boat would have to return to the *Taber* without any blubber to boil. But if the animal was shot so that it died immediately, collapsing at its position, the other walruses would simply lower their heads and resume sleeping. A skillful mate could kill walruses as quickly as he could reload. In a single nine-day stretch between June 24 and July 3, 1871, the *Taber* took 241 walruses.

Once the walruses were killed, the boatsteerer cut the hides into pieces on shore. Then the three men from the boat crew separated the hides and blubber from the carcass and set aside the hearts, livers, tongues, and other meat to later grind into sausages. They chopped the tusks out of the upper jaws.

Blubber, meat, and tusks from up to ten walruses could be loaded into a single boat for transport to the ship. If there were more, the *Taber* would sail closer to assist. Once carcasses and crew were all positioned on the ship's deck, the men used knives to remove blubber from the walruses' hides. The blubber was then chopped into smaller chunks on a large cutting table or in a mincing machine. After the minced blubber dried out, it was tossed into the tryworks to boil. The material had to be cooked slowly, in a method similar to that of whale blubber, and stirred constantly. If the process was hurried, or if the men were negligent in their care of it, the blubber would burn and discolor, lowering its market value.

In July, the fleet suffered its first shipwreck of the season. As the ships approached Saint Lawrence Bay, the bark *Oriole* was stove by ice. Sailors from several vessels rowed over to assist the *Oriole's* crew. They pumped water out of the hold as quickly as they could and tried to find the leak, but the vessel was too badly damaged for repair. The *Oriole's* gear was sold to the other captains, and the ship was abandoned. Its crew dispersed to work the other ships.

The thirty-nine remaining ships of the fleet, including the *Taber*, continued to inch through a narrow strip of clear water to the Chukchi Sea north of the Bering Strait. The ice appeared to be cooperating at last, and the captains ordered the men to cease their search for walruses. The hunt for whales commenced in earnest.

nine
Whales and Ice

A bowhead whale can grow up to sixty feet in length and can weigh more than one hundred tons. It is black in color except for a white covering on its lower jaw. The bowhead has a layer of blubber twenty inches thick and the longest baleen plates of any whale on earth. Their thick blubber and abundant baleen made them prime targets for whalers. The combined value of the oil and bone from an average-sized bowhead in 1871 was worth about $7,000 (approximately $95,000 in 2005 dollars).

Bowhead whales feed on plankton. An oily appearance on the sea indicates a large concentration of the tiny creatures. If the whalers found the plankton, they knew bowheads would not be far away.

Stivers and Briggs lowered their whaleboats each day and navigated into areas of open water still too narrow for the *Taber* to sail through, looking for plankton or other signs of whales. But after long hours of searching with no signs of the

This stamp from the Faroe Islands depicts a bowhead whale.

bowheads, the men returned to the ship. To Captain Packard it was an omen of a difficult hunting season to come. "I am sorry to say," he wrote on August 18, "that we are having hard luck. We were the first ship to get up to the ice and the first to lower for a whale, but have had hard luck. We had three whales last year at this time." Unlike the easy abundance of the previous two years, which allowed the *Taber* to head for Honolulu early in the season with a full cargo, the captain realized he would need to keep the ship and his men in the Arctic as long as possible in 1871. With the ice lingering far longer into the season than usual, it was not an optimistic thought.

Even though the *Taber* was having trouble finding whales, a few ships in the fleet were successful. Black, sooty smoke from other shipboard tryworks filled the Arctic sky. Captain Packard and his crew hoped that a strong northeastern storm would arrive and clear the ice enough to allow them to progress to Point Barrow. Whaling opportunities were always plentiful there.

By the end of the first week in August, the fleet had not sailed far into the Arctic. Tacking near the Alaskan shoreline, they confronted a frozen world. Massive amounts of the ship-crushing, hull-slashing, frozen sea loomed before them. "The ice fast on the shore and has not been broken up this summer," Stivers scribbled in his daily log. Whales were plentiful, though, and many ships successfully captured bowheads while they were delayed by ice near Wainwright Inlet.

The Arctic procedures for chasing, killing, and processing whales were similar to those used in warmer climates, although a few of the tools and some of the work techniques had to be modified to accommodate harsher environmental conditions. One of the most important tools in Arctic bowhead whaling was the bomb lance. First used in the 1850s, the bomb lance was a metal cylinder fired from a gun and had a range of about sixty feet. When skillfully used, the weapon could instantly kill a whale, and it reduced the chances that the animal would be able to reach refuge under the ice.

If a dying whale did manage to swim under ice, the men would attach their whale line to the *Taber* and use the windlass to haul the massive animal out. If the whale died a great distance away from the whaleship, men had to cut the carcass into pieces on the ice and haul blubber and baleen back section by section. The complexity of the work was increased by the Arctic's strong winds, blowing snows, blinding fogs, and bitter cold temperatures.

On August 10, a sailor from the shipwrecked *Japan* died. The *Taber's* crew finished their daily search for whales in their boats and then buried the unfortunate man on shore, between Wainwright Inlet and Point Belcher. Briggs was moved by the event to write a short eulogy to the seaman in his journal:

> In Memory
> Of Lewis Kenney who departed this life Thursday, August 10, 1871 at 12 noon. He was a native of London, England, aged twenty-four years or there about. He was one of the English Bark Japan crew that was wrecked in October last up here. We are now called upon to witness on this solemn occasion the last tribute and respect paid to our fellow mariner and may we all bear it in mind that we have all got to go that way sooner or later. And from leaving this world of trouble and woe he has entered into a heavenly mansion where love and peace forever reins. The deceased died of scurvy on the lungs. Oh death, where is thy sting? Oh grave, where is thy victory?

The day after the burial, sudden winds forced massive sections of ice to shift toward shore where twenty ships were anchored. The movement of ice was so rapid that the fleet did not have time to escape. Channels of clear water froze completely within minutes, stranding many surprised whaleboat crews more than six miles away from their ships.

"The ice closed up suddenly," reported one captain, "and we were forced to drag twenty-six boats over it. Fourteen boats were collected on a single cake at one time. Within half an hour from the time the ice began to move, we were solidly enclosed." Dozens of tired, cold sailors had to walk miles back to their ships, dragging their boats over uneven ice most of the distance.

The *Henry Taber* managed to safely maneuver away from the encroaching ice that day, but got trapped by it the next. "Ice coming in from the southwest," Stivers reported. "Got

As the Arctic ice began to close in around the fleet, the whaleships continued to hunt for whales. *(Courtesy of The Bridgeman Art Library)*

ship under way [but] went into the floe and made fast. The ice seems to be very much on the move."

Then, as quickly as the ice had started moving, it suddenly stopped. A dozen ships were able to inch their way up the coast in the remaining narrow strip of open water. The *Taber* was still trapped, however, and could not join them. Undeterred in their desire to hunt for whales, Stivers and Briggs continued to lower their whaleboats and followed whatever water passages they could find in the constant hope of capturing a whale.

A week later, the ice surrounding the *Taber* opened. "At 5 p.m.," Briggs noted, "we came out of the ice into clear water. The [bark] *Florida* came out just ahead of us." But the freedom to sail was temporary. All thirty-nine of the fleet's vessels were soon forced to anchor in a twenty-mile stretch of

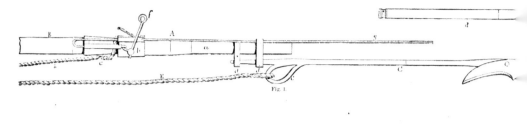

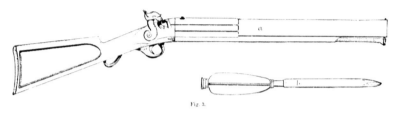

THE WHALE FISHERY.

1, Darting gun.   2, Cunningham and Cogan gun.   3, Brand muzzle-loading bomb-gun.   (Sect. v, vol. ii, pp. 253, 254.)

[See explanation on opposite page.]

The bomb lance was often employed in Arctic bowhead whaling to ensure a quick kill. *(Courtesy of the National Oceanic and Atmospheric Administration)*

water barely half a mile wide. The depth of sea water keeping the ships afloat only measured fourteen to twenty-four feet. The men heard many whales, but due to the heavy ice cover could not see them.

Within days the *Taber* was stuck again. Trying to dodge huge chunks of ice, the ship ran aground in shallow water. After several hours spent pumping water out of casks in the ship's hold to lighten it, the crew got the ship afloat once more.

For a few days, the weather was good and the whales were plentiful. The six-man crew of Briggs's starboard boat chased and killed a bowhead on the 25th. And although their boat was miles away from the *Taber* when the battle with the great whale ended, the men's spirits were high. Briggs fastened the dead animal to a cake of ice and returned to the *Taber*. Captain Packard carefully maneuvered the ship to the location of Briggs's catch and retrieved it for "cutting in."

Just as the men hoisted Briggs's whale to the ship's side and began removing its blubber, the *Taber* struck another section of ice. Several parts of the ship were badly damaged. "Got foul of a cake of ice," reported Briggs. "Broke our cutting stage bearers, slideboards. . . ." The crew stopped work on their whale to run a line of rope to a grounded piece of ice and with great effort, pulled the ship back into the water. They immediately returned to their work cutting-in and trying-out whale blubber.

Captain Packard realized that the amount of oil and bone removed from a single whale would not cover expenses of voyaging to the Arctic. He had to do something to ensure the ship could secure a profit when it returned to Honolulu that winter. He arranged with Captain Dean of the *John Wells* to "mate" the ships on August 28: Crews from the two vessels would work together to find, chase, and kill whales. The hunting range for each ship would be expanded and the odds for capturing a whale would increase. As a team, the *Taber* and *Wells* soon struck a bowhead and both ships equally divided the oil and baleen obtained.

As the crews of the *John Wells* and *Taber* were processing their combined whale catch, the *Contest* ran aground trying to maneuver away from the ice. Sailors from the *Oliver Crocker* and *Massachusetts* rushed over to assist in getting the ship into water again. Briggs entered the day's events in his logbook that night before falling into his bunk for a few hours sleep. He added an ominous remark at the end: "Weather as usual. Foggy. Three boats off whaling. Ice closing up."

On August 29, strong winds and blowing snows again advanced the ice dangerously close to the line of ships. It pushed so fast across remaining waterways that a third of the fleet became instantly trapped. The five most northern vessels, the *Roman*, *Comet*, *Concordia*, *Gay Head*, and *George* were hopelessly surrounded. The *Henry Taber*, *John Wells*, *Massachusetts*, *Contest*, *J.D. Thompson*, *Monticello*, *Elizabeth Swift*, and the *Fanny*, while not completely trapped, where unable to flee south to safety. With the exception of a narrow band of clear water where some of the ships were crowded against the shore, ice was the only thing anyone could see in every direction. Men stationed high in ships' riggings, and those trying to sleep in dark quarters below decks, listened as massive floes of deadly ice groaned and creaked around the wooden walls.

Combined efforts of several crews worked the *Fanny* clear of ice. The *Monticello* and *Elizabeth Swift* were also freed, but both immediately ran aground on a shoal in their efforts to escape. Crews from several ships, including the *Taber*, joined forces to shift the cargoes of the *Monticello* and *Elizabeth Swift* in the hope of getting the vessels afloat once more. Briggs noted that the wind was "all around the compass" and that it was "snowing like great guns" as they labored.

Captain Packard realized the situation had become dire: "Oh how many of this ship's company will live to see the last day of next August? God only knows. I will trust to his all wise hand." Even as ice continued its relentless advance toward shore where the ships were anchored, the seamen continued to whale. They warily rowed their boats around huge chunks of frozen sea in search of bowheads. When the ice was too thick to navigate around, the men simply dragged their boats across the top. Most maintained the optimistic belief that a strong northeaster storm would soon blow through and force the ice back as it had in past years.

The storm did not come.

ten
Shipwrecked

O n September 1, the crew of the *Roman* was cutting-in a whale when drift ice suddenly rammed
its way under the ship's hull, badly damaging its
side. The men raced off the vessel, and, within minutes, ice
lifted the entire ship into the air and then crushed it "like
an eggshell." Forty minutes after the *Roman* first made contact with ice, it was gone. Only a tiny portion of its timbers
remained above the frozen surface of the sea. Its crewmembers were quickly divided among the thirty nearby whaling
vessels, several finding shelter on the *Taber*. Still, whaling
continued.

On the second day of September, again without warning, the *Comet* was forced up and half out of the water. Its
crew abandoned it just as the ship was snapped in half by
two massive chunks of pressing ice. In hard snow with little
visibility, the *Comet's* crew members were divided among

By the start of September 1871, ships were being sunk or trapped by the ice on an almost daily basis.

the fleet. The same day, the *Thomas Dickason* reported capturing two whales.

The following three days continued the fleet's strange pattern of successful whale chases and devastating shipwrecks. On September 5th, first mate George Duffy of the bark *Seneca* entered in his ship's log that his vessel had struck a whale and commenced the cutting-in process. On the 6th, the *Eugenia* and *John Wells* were both irreparably damaged when driven aground by ice. On the 7th, the second mate of the *Emily Morgan* was killed when his bomb gun malfunctioned during a whale chase. Later that day, black smoke swirled from the deck of his ship as the *Emily Morgan's* crew rendered oil from the dead whale's blubber.

By September 8th, thirty-two ships were totally surrounded by ice. All exits out were gone. No one could continue to deny that an early winter had taken a brutal grip on the Arctic. All attempts at whaling ended.

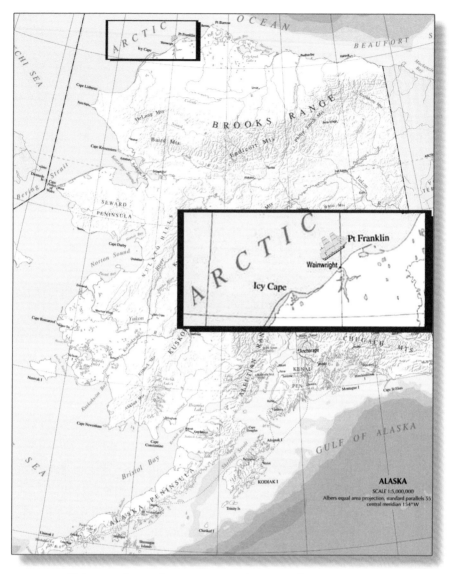

This map shows the approximate location of the stranded fleet.

"Some twenty-three ships in sight," wrote Stivers, "and nearly everyone in the fleet despairs of getting their ships south this fall. Which is a cause of much uneasiness."

Desperate questions raced from ship to ship. Were they trapped for the duration of the winter, or only for a few days?

100

How far did the ice extend? Was there clear water just beyond the fleet's limited view? And what about the seven unaccounted for whaling ships that had traveled into the Arctic with the fleet? Were they safe farther south, or already en route to safe harbors?

It was agreed that Captain Owen of the *Contest*, Captain Fisher of the *Oliver Crocker*, and Captain Dexter of the *Emily Morgan* would lead a small exploratory expedition of whaleboats through the remaining narrow channels of clear water near shore. They would determine the extent of ice and depth of sea south of the fleet's position and report back with a recommendation.

After many hours of rowing through increasingly icy passageways they found areas of water wide enough for the ships to navigate, but not deep enough for the ships' hulls to cross. There was less than nine feet of water in many places, and no more than four in others. Even if the fleet somehow managed to escape its immediate iced-in predicament, none of the vessels would be able to traverse the shallow seas beyond. The three commanders returned to the worried crews with the alarming news.

Gale-force winds howled through the whaleships' rigging as the helpless sailors watched and waited for a miracle. The storm brought rain, snow, sleet, and powerful winds from the south. Instead of forcing the frozen sea to retreat enough for the vessels to break free from their prison, it forced the ice to enclose them more tightly.

In a few short hours, ice drove upon the *Eugenia*, breaking its rudder. The *Awashonks* was crushed, the *Julian* severely damaged, and the *Elizabeth Swift* grounded. Thick fog developed as ice began to fill even the smallest sections of clear

This 1871 engraving depicts several ships forced out of the water by Arctic ice. *(Courtesy of The New Bedford Whaling Museum)*

water near the shore. First mate William Earle of the bark *Emily Morgan* wrote: "The sea . . . is one vast expanse of ice, not a speck of water to be seen."

"We felt keenly our responsibility," Captain Kelley later remembered, "with three million dollars worth of property and 1,200 lives at stake." He, along with Captain Williams of the *Monticello* and Captain Packard of the *Taber*, volunteered to lead a few whaleboats on a second expedition to the south. They planned to travel as far as possible through the remaining cracks in the ice to determine the fleet's exact location in relation to open ocean. Their hope for getting the ships out of the region was gone, but perhaps their crews and families could somehow escape the ice in the smaller, lighter whaleboats.

The three commanders battled their way through ten miles of narrow, meandering channels of icy water. They did not reach open sea and, with heavy hearts, returned to their ships. Captain Kelley later wrote, "The search for open water was in vain. We felt there was no possibility of rescue."

The whalers had not made contact with anyone in the outside world since they arrived at the edge of the Arctic pack ice five months earlier. No one would give thought to their well-being until they failed to sail their ships into port at Honolulu or San Francisco at the end of the season. Although more than 1,200 strong in number, they were helplessly isolated from the rest of the world. Without precedence to guide them and no one to turn to for help, the fleets' commanders were charged with a perilous decision: should they order their men to stay with ships or to abandon them?

A Benjamin Russell panorama of the ships involved in the 1871 disaster *(Courtesy of The New Bedford Whaling Museum)*

Staying would provide shelter against winter temperatures—likely to drop to fifty degrees below zero Fahrenheit. And there was still a chance, albeit a slim one, that winds from the northeast would blow through in the coming days and temporarily push the ice back long enough for the ships to escape.

But staying was a tremendous gamble. The ships were trapped far from any available harbor and would be exposed to every storm. If strong winds continued to come from any direction *except* the much-needed northeast, the entire fleet could be destroyed by crushing ice. And in the unlikely event that a few of the ships miraculously remained intact, they held food and heat-fuel to last only about ninety days. Without proper nourishment and clothing to endure the Arctic's nine-month-long winter season, a thousand people would die of starvation or exposure before spring.

Abandoning the whaling vessels and attempting escape on whaleboats through the swiftly disappearing channels of water seemed the more practical choice, but it was fraught with serious risks. No one knew how far the ice extended beyond the ten miles Captain Packard and the others had traversed. And if the boats *could* get to open ocean, where would they go after that? The nearest port would take at least six weeks to reach in a fully functional ship under excellent weather conditions. No one dared venture a guess at the amount of time it might require in small, aimlessly drifting boats fully dependent upon nature's mercy.

Unfortunately, with the ice closing in each passing hour, time for debate had run out. The commanders agreed that attempting to remain in the Arctic throughout the winter was not a wise option. But what was the safest way to leave?

Whaleboats were designed to accommodate only six men. More than a dozen people would have to be crammed into each one. Overburdened, the small vessels would be forced to ride dangerously low in the water. A sudden storm could easily plunge the helpless passengers into the cold sea. With temperatures so far below freezing and no way to get clothes dry or bodies warm, death seemed inevitable for many.

There was also the possibility that the channels would freeze before the boats reached the southern edge of the pack ice. If that happened, 1,200 people would be stranded in the ice, unable to maneuver their boats south or to easily return north to the stranded ships. The captains would have condemned their people to suffer nature's worst conditions without even the limited protection afforded by the shelter of the fleet.

Before they gave the order to abandon the ships, the desperate commanders agreed to one final experiment. They tried to lighten the *Kohola* and *Victoria*, the fleet's smallest ships, in the hope one of the two could somehow creep over the top of the land-water channel southbound. Casks of oil, barrels of provisions, and heavy equipment were hauled out of the vessels' holds and transferred to the decks of other ships. The crews labored shoulder-to-shoulder for hours, hopeful that if they could just get one of the ships free, a few men could go in search of help. Yet, even stripped bare, both the *Kohola* and *Victoria* remained too heavy for their hulls to clear the ice.

While the sailors struggled unsuccessfully to free the two ships, Captain D. R. Fraser of the *Florida* announced he would lead three whaleboats south, as previous commanders had done. This time, though, Captain Fraser was determined to continue even farther than previous expeditions. If he found the distance was not too great—and if the water route continued far enough—he and the other commanders would know that ordering their crews and families to abandon the fleet was the best decision.

Captain Fraser departed on September 10. While he was gone, the men he left behind prepared the whaleboats and provisions for the possibility of leaving. On the *Taber*, officers and crew worked side-by-side to boil beef and pork in the try-works, stow it in casks, and load them into the boats. Canvas bags were made for holding bread and other food. Boat bottoms were sheathed with copper, and false keels were added to keep the ice from cutting through the planking. Risers were built on the gunwales to increase the height of the boats' sides and boat covers and mounting boards were created to keep out as much sea water as possible. As hours turned into days, and Captain Fraser did not return, the men's hopes faded.

Finally, on September 12, Captain Fraser returned with incredible news. It had taken seventy miles of difficult rowing, but he had managed to follow channels of clear water all the way to open ocean. There he discovered two whaleships anchored just off Icy Cape. Five other vessels were caught in the ice near the cape but were working their way free.

Captain Fraser had raced to the ships and told them about the plight of the northern Arctic fleet. When one of the commanders, Captain Dowden of the bark *Progress*, learned of their dire circumstances, he said, "Tell them all I will wait for them as long as I have an anchor left or a spar to carry a sail."

The hopeful news alleviated doubts among the commanders. With each passing hour, ice was sealing off what remained of their final escape route. The fleet captains ordered the fleet abandoned and sent a few boats to the south loaded with provisions to sustain their shipwrecked men on the rescue vessels. A letter, written by Captain Henry Pease of the *Champion*, was also forwarded to the seven commanders of the rescue ships, imploring them to keep their promise to wait and lend aid:

> Gentlemen . . . Counting the crews of the four wrecked ships, we number some twelve hundred souls, with not more than three months' provisions and fuel, no clothing suitable for winter wear. An attempt to pass the winter here would be suicidal. Not more than two hundred out of the twelve hundred would survive to tell the tale. Looking at our deplorable situation squarely in the face, we feel convinced that to save the lives of our crews, a speedy abandonment of our ships is necessary.
>
> We . . . now call on you in the voice of humanity to abandon your whaling, sacrifice your personal interest, as well as that of your owners, and put your ships in condition to receive on board ourselves and crews for transit to some civilized port. We shall commence sending the sick and some provisions tomorrow. With small boats and nearly seventy miles to pull, we shall not be able to send much provision. Feeling confident that you will not abandon us, we are respectfully yours.
>
> (Signed Henry Pease, Jr. with thirty-one other masters.)

The commanders were concerned about saving the lives of their men and families, but they were also well aware of the financial implications of abandoning their ships. Leaving an entire fleet in the Arctic was without precedent. Never had so many ships been deserted in one place at one time. With twenty-one of the thirty-two vessels from New Bedford, Massachusetts, they realized the economic stability of the entire United States whaling industry would be adversely affected.

The commanders knew questions would arise when the story of the great whaleship disaster of 1871 reached investors and newspapers. Had the captains kept their ships in the Arctic too long? Did they leave too early? Should they have been whaling in the far northern reaches of the globe to begin with? If lives were lost in the struggle to get to the waiting ships, could they have been spared by different choices?

In an attempt to provide a unified answer to future questions, the captains held a final meeting on September 12 to sign a document outlining their reasons for leaving and their unanimous decision to abandon the ships by September 14:

> Point Belcher, Arctic Ocean
> September 12, 1871
> Know all men by these presents, that we, the undersigned, masters of whaleships, now lying at Point Belcher, after holding a meeting concerning our dreadful situation, have all come to the conclusion that our ships cannot be got out this year, and there being no harbor that we can get our vessels into, and not having provisions enough to feed our crews to exceed three months, and being in a barren country where there is neither food or fuel to be obtained, we feel ourselves under the painful necessity of abandoning our vessels, and trying to work our way south with our boats, and if possible to get on board of ships that are south of the ice. We think it would not be prudent to leave a single soul to look after our vessels, as the first westerly gale will crowd the ice ashore, and either crush the ships or drive them high upon the beach.
>
> Three of the fleet have already been crushed, and two are now lying hove out, which have been crushed by the ice, and are leaking badly. We have now five wrecked crews distributed among us. We have barely room to swing at anchor between the pack of ice and the beach, and are lying in three fathoms of water. Should we be cast upon the beach it would be at least eleven months before we could look for assistance, and in all

probability nine out of ten would die of starvation or scurvy before the opening of spring.

Therefore, we have arrived at these conclusions after the return of our expedition under command of Capt. D. R. Fraser of the *Florida*, he having with whaleboats worked to the southward as far as Blossom Shoals, and found that the ice pressed ashore the entire distance from our position to the Shoals, leaving in several places only sufficient depth of water for our boats to pass through, and this liable at any moment to be frozen over during twenty-four hours, which would cut off our retreat even by the boats, as Capt. Fraser had to work through a considerable quantity of young ice during his expedition, which cut up his boats badly.

The letter was signed by each commander. When Captain Packard returned with his order to abandon the *Henry Taber*, Stivers scrawled his final note in the ship's official logbook: "Boats are getting ready to journey south for our lives."

The sailors understood that deserting the fleet offered their only chance for survival. But leaving behind everything they had worked so hard to gain, on ships that had become their homes on the high seas, was difficult. William Fish Williams, a ten-year-old passenger on his father's doomed whaleship *Monticello*, later explained: "The usual abandonment of a ship is the result of some irreparable injury and is executed in great haste; but here we were leaving a ship that was absolutely sound, that had been our home for nearly ten months and had taken us safely through many a trying time."

Not certain of their destination or their survival, 1,219 men, women, and children huddled against each other in the cramped wooden whaleboats. William Earle of the *Emily Morgan* wrote he had a "sad heart ordering all the men into the boats and with a last look over the decks abandoned the ship to the mercy of the elements." As he rowed his boat through icy channels of water he realized: "All of the ships we passed were abandoned or their crews leaving in their boats. Hundreds of boats apparently were ahead of us as far as the eye could search."

A somber procession of nearly two hundred whaleboats eventually headed south in search of rescue. Briggs wrote on September 15: "We have left our home for parts unknown. So ends the log, journal, voyage and also the end of the bark *Henry Taber.*"

But the abandoned whaleships were not vacant for long. Shortly after the fleeing boats disappeared over the icy horizon, Eskimos boarded the vessels. They carried away most of the ships' planks, sails and rigging, bone, oil, and any

Several of the trapped whaleships were set ablaze by Eskimos after they were abandoned. *(Scala/Art Resource)*

food they could find. Many consumed deadly liquids from the ships' medicine chests. In retaliation for the sickness and deaths the misused medicines caused, the natives set several of the whaleships on fire.

Miles away from their once-proud vessels, the whalers discovered that ice had formed one solid body all the way to Icy Cape, leaving only a narrow strip of clear water close to land for the boats to use. It was arduous travel to avoid the cutting edges of the frozen sea, and by nightfall everyone was exhausted. "As night came on the winds increased and . . . darkness closed around us," remembered William Earle of the *Emily Morgan*. "Heavy, black clouds blew to rest over us and it was not possible to see more than a few feet and we were in constant danger of coming in collision with the many fragments of ice floating in the narrow passages between the land and the main pack."

Most of the refugees spent the night on the beach at Icy Cape instead of attempting to maneuver their boats around ice floes in the darkness. Tents were erected on shore and fires were built for cooking. Rain fell heavily and wind blew violently over the scattering of tents and people.

The next morning everyone climbed back into their boats and resumed the search for the rescue ships to the south. After several hours of rowing and sailing, the boats finally reached ice-free water. But their troubles were not over.

The dangers of Arctic ice, which had challenged the men's seamanship and threatened their lives, was finally behind them, but they were now exposed to the brutal battering of the rough, wind-driven open ocean. The overloaded whaleboats tossed dangerously in the rolling seas. The boats rode so low the men had to constantly bail out water to keep

This print depicts the whaleship refugees spending the night on Icy Cape during their pilgrimage south to the rescue ships. *(Courtesy of The New Bedford Whaling Museum)*

them afloat and clothing was saturated with freezing brine. Carefully packed bread and flour was spoiled.

All eyes frantically searched the horizon for the ships that had promised to wait. Everyone knew that finding a few vessels on a vast expanse of ocean would require all the luck they had left.

Just as hope was beginning to fade once more, someone spotted the dark silhouette of a ship in the distance. Then another, and another. As promised, seven whaleships were clear of ice and waiting.

After more than seventy miles of rowing and sailing, the boats finally reached open water.

The *Europa, Daniel Webster, Midas, Arctic, Progress, Lagoda,* and *Chance* were straining against their anchors in order to hold their positions in the strong winds and seas. J. B. Ellis, mate on the rescue whaleship *Lagoda,* reported in his log on September 16: "This day commences with fresh breezes from the southeast with rain and fog. Bark under all sail working towards the land. At 10 a.m. came to anchor close to those ships that are taking the wrecked men on board. All hands employed getting on board wrecked men and provisions. Wind increasing. . . ."

With rescue so near, there was one final hurtle for the shipwrecked survivors to overcome. Deep rolling waves posed a danger to everyone as they struggled to climb from the small bobbing boats onto the large swaying ships. The small boats banged against the ships' sides, seemingly determined to crush anyone who became wedged between the two.

A print showing the overcrowded whaleboats making their way out to the rescue ships *(Courtesy of The New Bedford Whaling Museum)*

Women in long skirts, and children (one an infant), fought to climb aboard the rescue ships—a challenging task for even the most experienced sailors. The barks *Arctic*, *Midas*, and *Progress* each lost an anchor trying to hold their positions long enough in the powerful winds to get the survivors on board. Incredibly, by September 17, the crews of the seven ships had successfully pulled every desperate person onto their decks without the loss of a single life.

Although each of the ships were built to accommodate forty or fewer men, the *Europa* crowded 280 of the survivors within its decks, the *Arctic* 250, the *Progress* 221, *Lagoda* 195, *Daniel Webster* 113, *Midas* one hundred and *Chance* sixty. Captain Dowden of the *Progress* gave his small cabin to the three captains who had their wives and children with them. "Everybody was provided for," wrote young William

Fish Williams, "except Captain Dowden, and I never did know where he managed to get his sleep."

The small whaleboats that brought the survivors to safety were then sent adrift. There was no room to store them on the overburdened whaleships. The seven ships then weighed anchor and headed southwest. After a stop at Plover Bay for extra water and wood, all sails were set for the six-week journey to the safe harbor at Honolulu.

eleven

Homeward Bound

N ews of the whaleship disaster did not reach newspapers until weeks after the fleet had been abandoned and its crewmembers had been rescued. But once the story hit newspapers it spread throughout the world. At the comfort of kitchen tables in sunny Honolulu, and stretched out in front of warming fires in New England, the whalers' frightening travails, and their amazing tale of survival, made dramatic reading. Forty ships had sailed into the Arctic that year, but only seven sailed out. A few men had perished during the long voyage across the North Pacific bound for Honolulu, but not a single loss of life in the Arctic was reported.

Abram Briggs's escape from Icy Cape to Honolulu on the whaleship *Europa* took one month and nine days. "All hands on shore," he wrote when the ship reached Oahu on October 24, 1871. After months working and living in the Arctic's ice, snow, fog, and wind, followed by nearly six weeks of cramped living within the confines of the small rescue whale-ship, Honolulu's warm breezes and sandy beaches were a welcome sight. "Our trials and troubles of the Arctic Ocean are over," he wrote.

Problems for the United States Consulate in Honolulu, however, had only begun. The whaleships *Arctic*, *Progress*, and *Midas* arrived in the Hawaiian port on October 23, 1871. The *Lagoda*, *Daniel Webster*, and *Europa* all dropped anchor on the 24th. The *Chance* arrived, leaking badly, on the 29th.

United States maritime law stated that when shipwrecked in a foreign land, every American seaman was entitled to receive aid from the nearest United States consulate. Honolulu was not yet part of the United States, so the consulate there was required to provide food, shelter, and clothing to the unprecedented number of destitute mariners.

Nearly four hundred of the men who climbed off the rescue whaleships were natives of the South Pacific Islands and did not qualify for American aid. They went home or signed on to crew other vessels. But almost eight hundred eligible men remained, and most wanted to get home to New England. They were filthy and hungry. They had no money, no food, and no possessions except the dirty, worn-out clothing they had worn for two months. One hundred of the men were sick and needed immediate medical treatment.

The recently hired United States Consul, C. S. Mattoon, and his clerk worked day and night, almost without stop, to arrange for the men to receive food and shelter and to somehow obtain passage home. When the steamship *Moses Taylor* cleared for San Francisco on October 25, Mattoon used the consulate's funds to arrange for thirty of the officers, including Captain

Timothy Packard, first mate John Stivers, and the officers traveling with families, to obtain passage. A week later, the San Francisco-based bark *D.C. Murray* also departed carrying several others.

The rest of the men were temporarily housed at Honolulu's "Sailor's Home" (a boardinghouse for visiting seamen) or given shelter at the island's United States Marine Hospital. The hospital was operated by Dr. John McGrew. The doctor had been a surgeon in the Army during the Civil War and had experience dealing with a large number of men on short notice.

With their basic needs met, Mattoon knew he needed more money if he was to get the huge number of jobless, restless men off the ill-prepared island. Communication between Mattoon's consulate in Hawaii and the United States government in Washington, D.C., that had authority over his office and all of his funds did not have the benefit of electronic mail, telephones, or even telegraphs. Mattoon had to handwrite a letter to the assistant secretary of the United States informing him of the whaleship disaster and asking for financial assistance. His letter left on a steamship headed for California.

While awaiting the assistant secretary's reply, Mattoon tried to negotiate a government contract with three American merchant ships, *Ceylon*, *Powhattan*, and *Delaware*, anchored in Honolulu's harbor. He hoped to have them transport the remaining six hundred mariners to ports in the United States. The *Ceylon* and the *Powhattan* offered to ship the men home for forty dollars each in United States gold coin (Mattoon had hoped to secure passage for less than twenty dollars per man). The captains of the two vessels stipulated that the consulate should furnish all bedding, tin pots, pans, knives, forks, and spoons needed by the seamen during their voyages. Mattoon knew the extraordinary stipulations and exorbitant fees would cost the United States government thousands of dollars and had no choice but to refuse the demands.

Mattoon's only remaining option was to continue to send the wrecked seamen home a few at a time on willing vessels. He succeeded in shipping approximately half of the men to the United States by the end of the year. Another one hundred and fifty sailors found jobs on outbound vessels or as laborers on sugar plantations in the Islands. The last of those desperate to get home finally found passage out of Honolulu in April 1872.

The United States government's responsibility to the wrecked seamen ended as soon as they were delivered to American soil. Those arriving in San Francisco, regardless of rank or need, had to manage the remainder of their journeys home on their own. Many of the men, having lost their means to earn money months earlier, did not have the ability to feed themselves, much less secure train passage across the United States. San Francisco newspapers brought the plight of the destitute sailors to the attention of readers, imploring people to help the poor men.

Luckier than most, Captain Timothy Packard and First Mate John Stivers arrived in San Francisco the first week of November. The United States' first transcontinental railroad system had been completed two years earlier, and they purchased tickets for the east coast on the Central Pacific Railroad. Captain Packard arrived in New Bedford November 15, and Stivers continued on to his hometown of Stonington, Massachusetts.

While the *Henry Taber's* captain and first mate were reuniting with family and friends in New England that Thanksgiving, Abram Briggs was still awaiting his opportunity for passage out of Honolulu. On November 22, the *Moses Taylor* was preparing to depart Hawaii once more for California, and Mattoon secured passage for Briggs and several others.

The *Moses Taylor* arrived in San Francisco on December 4, 1871. Briggs immediately went to the west coast offices maintained by *Taber, Gordon, & Company,* the owners of the *Henry Taber*, to get his paycheck for the percentage of whale oil and baleen the *Taber* had accumulated prior to setting sail on its final, fateful voyage to the Arctic. He used his meager earnings to buy a ticket on the Central Pacific Railroad, as Captain Packard and John Stivers had done the month prior, and started his twelve-day journey across the United States to New Bedford. He arrived on December 16, "safe and sound."

With no loss of life reported, newspaper articles focused on the financial implications of the whaleship disaster. Overall investment in the western Arctic whaling fleet of 1871 was estimated at more than $1.5 million, equivalent to approximately $22 million in 2005. From the records kept for each voyage, approximately 13,665 barrels of whale oil, 965 barrels of sperm oil and 100,000 pounds of bone had been left behind on the ships when they were abandoned. The New Bedford citizens who had invested in the whaling ventures, as well as those who supplied and serviced the vessels when they returned to home port, suddenly faced financial losses on a scale never before encountered.

As the captains of the Arctic fleet of 1871 had expected, questions arose among the ships' owners and insurers about their decision to abandon the ships. Did the whaling captains panic and desert the fleet too soon? Could the captains have done anything to prevent the loss of so many ships and such valuable cargo? Was the Arctic too dangerous and unpredictable to merit future risks on whaling ventures? The wisdom of sailing ships into the Arctic, and the choices made in 1871 in particular, continued to be debated in insurance offices and harborside taverns for months.

Newspaper editorials around the country also fueled discussions. the *New York Times* reflected critical attitudes of many in the whaling industry who had lost significant money in the abandonment by claiming, "It is supposed that, spurred on by the successes of the last two years, and the temptation to hold on for a large catch at the last hour, the whalers became too venturesome, and hence suffered the terrible calamity."

But the editor of Honolulu's *Friend* newspaper reminded readers: "It is an easy matter in Honolulu, with the thermometer at eighty degrees, to criticize the actions of men who have faced danger and starvation under the shadow of icebergs. . . . The idea that thirty-three ship masters and their crews [including the bark *Oriole*] abandoned their ice-bound vessels, except from stern and dire necessity is not to be entertained for one moment."

While the whalers' courage and judgment was deliberated, the financial impact was not. As home port for twenty-one of the lost ships, New Bedford suffered more than any other city. The local newspaper, the *Republic Standard*, reported on November 9, 1871: "This is the severest blow which has ever fallen upon our leading business. Our best vessels and a very large amount of capital have been swept away in a single season, and it will take our city many years to recover from the effects of this disaster."

The *New York Times* continued to analyze the important event for the rest of the nation. The whaling disaster, the prestigious newspaper reported, "has seriously damaged, if it has not crippled, [New Bedford's] leading insurance offices [and] completely unsettled the oil market." The newspaper compared the effects of the disaster to the massive fire that spread through the city of Chicago on October 8, 1871. It was an exaggeration, of course. The Chicago fire killed nine hundred Chicagoans, left 90,000 people homeless, and resulted in $200 million in property loss, but the comparison served to heighten the public's curiosity.

A few entrepreneurs, however, were more curious about what could be gained from the disaster than what had been lost. What had happened to the ships after the whalemen abandoned them? Had every ship been crushed beyond salvage, or were some still intact and seaworthy? Were any still loaded with valuable oil and baleen, just waiting to bring fortune to someone industrious enough to return to the Arctic and retrieve them?

Captain Thomas Williams of the abandoned whaleship *Monticello* decided the possibility of instant fortune was worth pursuing. Within months after fleeing the Arctic with his wife and three children in his doomed ship's whaleboat, Captain Williams gathered a small group of investors in San Francisco to finance his return. His plan was to sail back to the region of the *Florence* and salvage as much oil, baleen, and ivory as he could. Captain Elijah Smith (who had been master of the abandoned *Carlotta*) and a Captain Jacobsen also shared the same idea. In early spring of 1872, the three ship commanders began a race northbound to salvage what remained of the wreckage.

Captain Williams and his crew of salvagers on the *Florence* arrived at the site of the disaster first. They found

Captain Thomas Williams *(Courtesy of The New Bedford Whaling Museum)*

several ships, most unrecognizable, scattered in pieces on the shore and ice. Only the *Minerva* appeared seaworthy.

Incredibly, many containers of oil and bundles of baleen remained intact, some still stowed in the broken holds of the wrecked ships. Others had washed up on shore. Captain Williams ordered his men to gather all of the undamaged casks and bundles they could find. With a cargo of 1,300 barrels of salvaged whale oil, $10,000 of baleen, and several containers of walrus oil, Captain Williams triumphantly prepared the *Minerva* and *Florence* to sail towards San Francisco.

Before the two ships departed, though, the captain made another discovery. An unnamed boatsteerer, from the original 1871 fleet, had sneaked back to the ships after they were abandoned instead of fleeing to the south with the other men. The man had attempted to live on the vessels throughout the winter and was in very poor physical condition when Captain Williams found him. However, he was able to report that two weeks after the crews had abandoned the fleet, a strong northeast gale pushed the ice back far enough to have permitted most of the ships to sail safely out of the Arctic. Shortly afterward, however, another gale had blown through, causing the unattended vessels to crash into the ice, shore, and each other. Apparently, if the captains had waited two weeks longer before ordering their men to flee to the south, they might have saved their ships and most of their cargo.

The losses in the Arctic in 1871 and debates about what should have happened did not deter other whalers from sailing to the region. There was still a market for whale oil, although petroleum was slowly replacing it as the world's illuminate and lubricant. And since experiments with strong, flexible plastics were in still in the initial phases of development, manufactures were willing to pay extraordinary prices for the multipurpose baleen. Baleen from one bowhead had increased in value to nearly $5,000 in 1878 (equaling about $90,000 in 2005).

For many whaleship captains and investors, whaling in the Arctic continued to be the fastest, most dependable way to earn a living and to make a profit. For them, the loss of so many whaleships in 1871 meant fewer competitors in the hunt for the diminishing populations of whales. Each spring following the disaster, whalers continued to gather at the edge of the pack ice and await their opportunity to challenge the Arctic.

But, just as the great whaleship disaster of 1871 was fading from everyone's memory, another catastrophe in the Arctic befell the whaling industry. In 1876, winter ice again formed fast and early. This time it trapped twelve ships. Unlike the disaster five years earlier, fifty-four crewmembers of the 1876 fleet did not flee their iced-in ships. They believed the fleet was being abandoned too early and probably hoped to sail their vessels out of Arctic waters as soon as weather and ice permitted.

Nine months later, whaleships entering the Arctic for the 1877 season made a terrible discovery. Only two of the fifty-four men were found alive. Two others had died while in the care of native villagers at Point Barrow. The remaining fifty men were never found.

The great whaleship disaster of 1871, coupled with the additional losses of life and property suffered in 1876, did not end American whaling, but the tragic events did hasten

In 1876, twelve ships attempted to spend the winter in the Arctic waters after getting trapped in the ice.

the industry's decline. Instead of reinvesting the insurance money awarded from the loss of Arctic whaling ships into new ones, New England capitalists shifted their funds to New Bedford's growing textile mill industries, manufacturing facilities, and other non-whaling ventures such as railroads and mining. By the mid-1870s, cotton textile manufacturing had become economically more important than whaling.

American workers embraced the new job opportunities afforded by mills and other land-based industries. New England cotton and woolen mills promised workers dependable pay and predictable work hours that life at sea could not offer. Long shifts at local factories near home were welcome alternatives to months spent in the confines of cramped, filthy

Cotton mills provided steady work that was relatively safe compared to the dangers of whaling. *(Library of Congress)*

ships' quarters. By 1880, only one-third of the 4,000 men who signed on to crew New Bedford whaleships were American citizens. Portuguese sailors made up another third, and the rest hailed from countries scattered around the globe.

The fate of the *Henry Taber's* crew also reflected America's gradual transition from sea-based pursuits to land-based endeavors. A few of the men, of course, returned to the sea on whaleships. When the *Eliza Adams* departed New Bedford's harbor on June 10, 1872, John Stivers was listed as the ship's first mate, and Abram Briggs had signed on as its fourth.

But for men like Captain Timothy C. Packard, the future

By the turn of the twentieth century, the whaling industry was in severe decline as America transitioned to more land-based business pursuits. *(Courtesy of The New Bedford Whaling Museum)*

belonged on shore. After twenty-one years living and working on the high seas, the thirty-six-year-old whaleship commander returned home to stay. He took a job as night watchman for the city of New Bedford and was nearby when his wife Phebe gave birth to three more children. He was home when his oldest daughter, Fanny, celebrated her fifteenth birthday and applied for her first job at a New Bedford woolen mill. He was also around to ensure that young Timothy Jr. signed up for school each year—not as a cabin boy on one of the few remaining whaleships, searching for fortune in the cold Arctic.

Timeline

1750s American whaleships begin sailing to South Atlantic.

1790s Whaleships venture into the Pacific Ocean.

1819 First American whaleships reach Hawaii.

1848 The *Superior* becomes first whaleship to cross Bering Strait.

1868 Whaleship *Henry Taber* departs New Bedford, Massachusetts.

1870 Whaleship *Japan* disappears while whaling in Arctic.

1871 MAY–JUNE
      Forty whaleships, including *Henry Taber*, sail into Arctic waters to hunt walrus and bowhead whales.
      JUNE
      Survivors of whaleship *Japan* rescued.
      JULY
      Whaleship *Oriole* destroyed by Arctic ice.
      AUGUST
      Ice closes in around northern Arctic whaling fleet.
      SEPTEMBER
      Thirty-two whaleships abandoned near Point Belcher.
      OCTOBER
      The first of seven rescue ships begins arriving at

Honolulu with shipwrecked crews on board.

Officers of *Henry Taber* return home.

1872   One whaleship salvaged from abandoned fleet.

1876   Twelve whaleships lost near Point Barrow; fifty-two lives lost.

1921   Last bowhead whale taken by commercial whaleship.

Sources

CHAPTER TWO: Leaving New Bedford

p. 17, "the dearest place to . . ." Herman Melville, *Moby Dick* (New York: Penguin, 1961), 50.

p. 17-18, "All these brave houses . . ." Ibid., 50.

p. 21, "Everyone knows what a . . ." Ibid., 106.

p. 26, "with a beautiful breeze . . ." Captain Timothy C. Packard, *On the bark* Henry Taber *of New Bedford* (Providence Public Library, Providence, RI: Microfilm #317), 23 October 1868.

CHAPTER THREE: Captain and Crew

p. 28, "In most American whaleships . . ." Melville, *Moby Dick*, 157.

p. 35, "black and slimy with . . ." J. Ross Browne, *Etchings of a Whaling Cruise*, (Cambridge, MA: Harvard University Press, 1968), 24.

p. 36, "We are living pretty . . ." Packard, *On the bark*, 30 November 1868.

p. 37, "The captain is getting . . ." Abram Briggs, *A Journal kept by A.G. Briggs of the Bk.* Henry Taber*, Sailed Oct. 23, 1868, Bound to the N.W.* (Kendall Research Library, New Bedford, MA: Microfilm #133, log #801), 31 January 1869.

p. 39, "Today all hands are . . ." John Stivers, *Logbook of the bark* Henry Taber*, 1868-1871*, (Kendall Research

Library, New Bedford, MA: Microfilm #282), 21 December 1868.

CHAPTER FOUR: Life at Sea

p. 40, "We find that our little bark can sail . . ." Packard, *On the bark,* 24 November 1868.

p. 40-41, "I sprang up on . . ." Browne, *Etchings*, 28.

p. 41, "Nothing in sight but . . ." Stivers, *Logbook*, 17 January 1869.

p. 42, "For the most part . . ." Melville, *Moby Dick*, 159.

p. 45, "sent to the masthead . . ." Stivers, *Logbook*, 18 July 1869.

p. 46, "Called all hands at . . ." Packard, *On the bark*, 21 July 1869.

p. 46-47, "caught the three men . . ." Briggs, *A Journal*, 8 March 1869.

p. 49, "I can not see . . ." Packard, *On the bark*, 19 November 1869.

p. 49, "The fact that the . . ." Thomas Adamson, *Dispatches of the United States Consulate in Honolulu,* (Washington, D.C.: National Archives and Records Administration, Microfilm #144, Vol. 11), 31 December 1869.

p. 50, "Something tells me in . . ." Briggs, *A Journal*, 8 April 1869.

CHAPTER FIVE: The Floating Factory

p. 51, "Nothing in sight." Stivers, *Logbook*, 17 January 1869.

p. 55-56, "I often think that . . ." Enoch Carter Cloud, *Life on a Whale Ship: 1851-1854* (Wakefield, RI: Moyer Bell, 1994), 224.

p. 60, "I thought it was . . ." Harold Williams, ed., *One Whaling Family* (Boston: Houghton Mifflin, 1964), 25.

p. 60-61, "The smell of the . . ." Lisa Norling, *Captain Ahab Had a Wife* (Chapel Hill: University of North Carolina Press, 2000), 249.

p. 61, "A trying-out scene . . ." Browne, *Etchings*, 63.

CHAPTER SIX: Troubles in the Pacific

p. 64, "We cannot take any . . ." Packard, *On the bark*, 27 September 1869.

p. 66-67, "A Happy New Year . . ." Briggs, *A Journal*, 1 January 1871.

p. 68, "to the forecastle for. . ." Stivers, *Logbook*, 31 March 1871.

CHAPTER SEVEN: Gathering of the Arctic Fleet

p. 74, "the system of watches . . ." Margaret S. Creighton, "The Captain's Children: Life in the Adult World of Whaling, 1852-1907," *American Neptune Journal* 38, (1978): 216.

p. 75, "Father, dear Father, come . . ." Packard, *On the bark*, 25 June 1869.

p. 78, "Arctic ice isn't like . . ." Captain Hartson H. Bodfish, *Chasing the Bowhead* (Cambridge, MA: Harvard University Press, 1936), 41-42.

CHAPTER EIGHT: Early Warning

p. 81-82, "The gale blew harder . . ." Captain Frederick Barker, *Wreck of the Whaleship Japan* (New Bedford, MA: Republican Standard), 23 November 1871.

p. 82, "The air was piercing . . ." Ibid.

p. 82, "rendered me nearly desperate . . ." Barker, *Journal of the Whaleship Japan* (Kendall Research Library, New Bedford, MA: Microfilm #115, Log #866A): 8 October 1870-12 May 1871.

p. 82, "Let us hope . . . the Arctic Ocean." Briggs, *A Journal*, 20 June 1871.

p. 83, "all laid up with . . ." Stivers, *Logbook*, 1 July 1871.

p.85-86, "Should I ever come . . ." John R. Bockstoce, *Whales, Ice, and Men: The History of Whaling in the Western Arctic* (Seattle: University of Washington Press, 1986), 136.

CHAPTER NINE: Whales and Ice

p. 90, "I am sorry to . . ." Packard, *On the bark*, 18 August 1871.

p. 91, "The ice fast on . . ." Stivers, *Logbook*, 7 August 1871.

p. 92, "In memory of Lewis . . ." Briggs, *A Journal*, 10 August 1871.

p. 92, "The ice closed up . . ." Everett Allen, *Children of the Light: the Rise and Fall of New Bedford Whaling and the Death of the Arctic Fleet* (Boston: Little, Brown, and Co., 1973), 215.

p. 92-93, "Ice coming in from . . ." Stivers, *Logbook*, 12 August 1871.

p. 93-94, "At 5 p.m. we came . . ." Briggs, *A Journal,* 17 August 1871.

p. 95, "Got foul of a . . ." Ibid., 27 August 1871.

p. 95, "Weather as usual. Foggy . . ." Ibid., 28 August 1871.

p. 96, "all around the compass," Ibid., 30 August 1871.

p. 96, "snowing like great guns," Ibid., 31 August 1871.

p. 96, "Oh how many of . . ." Packard, *Bark Henry Taber: Aug. 18, 1871-Sept. 5, 1871* (Kendall Research Library, New Bedford Whaling Museum, New Bedford, MA: Log #455), 31 August 1871.

CHAPTER TEN: Shipwrecked

p. 98, "like an eggshell." "Sad News from the Arctic Ocean" (New Bedford, MA: *Republican Standard*), November, 9, 1871.

p. 100, "Some twenty-three ship . . ." Stivers, *Logbook*, 7 September 1871.

p. 102, "The sea . . . to be seen." William Earle, *Logbook of the Emily Morgan*, (New Bedford Free Public Library, New Bedford, MA: Microfilm #23), 9 September 1871.

p. 102, "We felt keenly our . . ." Allen, *Children of the Light*, 231.

p. 103, "The search for open . . ." Ibid., 235.

p. 106, "Tell them all I . . ." Bockstoce, *Whales, Ice, and Men*, 156.

p. 107, "Gentlemen . . . Counting the crews . . ." *Claims for the Bringing Home of the Wrecked Crews of the Arctic Whaleships* (New Bedford, MA: Whalemen's Shipping List and Merchants Transcript), 26 March 1872.

p. 108-109, "Know all men by . . ." Briggs, *A Journal*, back pages of logbook.

p. 109, "Boats are getting ready . . ." Stivers, *Logbook*, 13 September 1871.

p. 109, "The usual abandonment of . . ." Williams, *One Whaling Family*, 238.

p. 109-110, "sad heart ordering all . . ." Earle, *Emily Morgan*, 14 September 1871.

p. 110, "We have left our . . ." Briggs, *A Journal*, 15 September 1871.

p. 111, "As night came on . . ." Earle, *Emily Morgan*, 14 September 1871.

p. 113, "This day commences with . . ." J.B. Ellis, *Log of the Lagoda* (Kendall Research Library, New Bedford

Whaling Museum, New Bedford, MA: Microfilm #277, log #494), 16 September 1871.

p. 114-115, "Everybody was provided for . . ." Williams, *One Whaling Family*, 239.

CHAPTER ELEVEN: Homeward Bound

p. 116-117, "All hands on shore . . ." Briggs, *A Journal*, 24 October 1871.

p. 117, "Our trials and troubles . . ." Ibid.

p. 120, "safe and sound," Ibid., 16 December 1871.

p. 122, "It is supposed that . . ." "Loss of the Arctic Fleet," *New York Times*, November 7, 1871.

p. 122, "It is an easy matter . . ." *We Left Not One Minute Too Soon* (Honolulu, HI: The Friend), 9 November 1871.

p. 122, "This is the severest . . ." *Our Calamity* (New Bedford, MA: Republican Standard), 9 November 1871.

p. 122, "has seriously damaged, if . . ." "Loss of the Arctic Fleet," *New York Times, 7 November 1871.*

Bibliography

Adamson, Thomas. "Dispatches of the United States Consulate in Honolulu," Washington, D.C.: National Archives and Records Administration Microfilm #144, Vol. 11, December 31, 1869.

Allen, Everett. *Children of the Light: The Rise and Fall of New Bedford Whaling and the Death of the Arctic Fleet.* Boston: Little, Brown, and Co., 1973.

Barker, Frederick. *Journal of the Whaleship Japan.* New Bedford, MA: Kendall Research Library, Microfilm #115, Log #866A, October 8, 1870-May 12, 1871.

———. "Wreck of the Whaleship Japan." *Republican Standard*, November 23, 1871.

Bockstoce, John R. *Whales, Ice, and Men: The History of Whaling in the Western Arctic.* Seattle: University of Washington Press, 1986.

Bodfish, Hartson H. *Chasing the Bowhead.* Cambridge, MA: Harvard University Press, 1936.

Briggs Abram. *A Journal kept by A.G. Briggs of the Bk. Henry Taber, Sailed Oct. 23, 1868, Bound to the N.W.* New Bedford, MA: Kendall Research Library Microfilm #133, log #801, January 31, 1869.

Browne, J. Ross. *Etchings of a Whaling Cruise.* Cambridge, MA: Harvard University Press, 1968.

"Claims for the Bringing Home of the Wrecked Crews of the Arctic Whaleships." New Bedford, MA: *Whalemen's Shipping List and Merchants Transcript,* March 26, 1872.

Cloud, Enoch Carter. *Life on a Whale Ship: 1851-1854.* Wakefield, RI: Moyer Bell, 1994.

Creighton, Margaret S. "The Captain's Children: Life in the Adult World of Whaling, 1852-1907." *American Neptune Journal* 38 (1978).

Earle, William. *Logbook of the Emily Morgan.* New Bedford, MA: New Bedford Free Public Library Microfilm #23, September 9, 1871.

Ellis, J.B. *Log of the Lagoda.* New Bedford, MA: Kendall Research Library Microfilm #277, log #494, September 16, 1871.

"Loss of the Arctic Fleet." *New York Times,* November 7, 1871.

Melville, Herman. *Moby Dick.* New York: Penguin, 1961.

Norling, Lisa. *Captain Ahab Had a Wife.* Chapel Hill, NC: University of North Carolina Press, 2000.

"Our Calamity." *Republican Standard,* November 9, 1871.

Packard, Timothy C. *Bark Henry Taber: Aug. 18, 1871- Sept. 5, 1871.* New Bedford, MA: New Bedford Whaling Museum, Log #455, August 31, 1871.

———. *On the bark Henry Taber of New Bedford.* Providence, RI: Providence Public Library Microfilm #317, November 23, 1868.

"Sad News from the Arctic Ocean." *Republican Standard*, November 9, 1871.

Stivers, John. *Logbook of the bark Henry Taber, 1868-1871*. New Bedford, MA: Kendall Research Library Microfilm #282, December 21, 1869.

"We Left Not One Minute Too Soon." *The Friend*, November 9, 1871.

Williams, Harold, ed. *One Whaling Family*. Boston: Houghton Mifflin, 1964.

Web sites

The New Bedford Whaling Museum
http://www.whalingmuseum.com

The New Bedford Whaling Museum Web site features numerous articles about the history of whaling and the town of New Bedford. It also has an online archive of images from the whaling area, as well as information about visiting the museum.

International Whaling Commission
http://www.iwcoffice.org

The homepage of the International Whaling Commission offers information on the history of whaling, contemporary debates over the ethics of whaling, and the conservation of whales. Visitors to the site can also find facts about different whale species, including the sperm and baleen whales. Also features links to other international sites concerned with whaling in contemporary society.

Greenpeace
**http://www.greenpeace.org/international/campaigns/
save-our-seas-2/save-the-whales**
Greenpeace Web site devoted to ending the whaling industry in the 21st century and preserving the lives of whales on the planet. Information about contemporary whaling, as well as links and information for those who are opposed to it.

Index

Adamson, Thomas, 49-50

American Civil War, 18,
    42, 50, 118

Arctic (whaleship), 113-
    114, 117,

Awashonks (whaleship), 101

Barker, Captain Frederick,
    70, 80-82, *81*, 85-86

Benecke, Heinrich, 23,
    45-46, 49

Briggs, Abram, 23, 25, 34,
    37, 43, 45-47, 50, 52-54,
    56, 61-62, 66-67, 71, 75-
    76, 82, 89, 92-96, 110,
    116-117, 120, 128

Browne, J. Ross, 61

Bullock, Warren, 23

Carlotta (whaleship), 124

Ceylon (merchant ship), 118

Champion (whaleship), 107

Chance (whaleship), 113-114

Comet (whaleship), 96, 98

Concordia (whaleship),
    71, 96

Contest (whaleship, 71,
    95-96, 101

Daniel Webster (whaleship),
    113-114, 117

D.C. Murray (steamship), 118

Dean, Captain, 95
Delaware (merchant ship),
   118
Dexter, Captain, 101
Dowden, Captain, 106, 115
Duffy, George, 99

Earle, William, 102, 109-111,
Edwards, David, 23, 52
Eliza Adams (whaleship),
   128
Elizabeth Swift (whaleship),
   71, 96, 101
Ellis, J.B., 113
Ellis, John, 23
Emily Morgan (whaleship),
   72, 99, 101, 109, 111
Eugenia (whaleship), 99, 101
Europa (whaleship), 113-
   114, 116-117

Fanny (whaleship), 71-72,
   96
Fisher, Captain, 101
Florida (whaleship), 12-13,
   105-106, 109
Fraser, Captain D.R., 105-
   106, 109

Gay Head (whaleship),
   71, 96
George Howland (whaleship),
   71, 96

Gibbin, Edward, 23
Grant, Ulysses S., 42

Henry Taber (whaleship),
   11-13, 18-20, 22-26, 27-
   30, 33-39, 40-48, 50, 51-
   52, 54, 57-58, 60, 63,
   64, 66-68, 71-72, 74, 79-
   82, 86-88, 89-96, 98, 1
   02, 106, 109-110, 120,
   127

Jacobsen, Captain, 124
Japan (whaleship), 70, 80-
   83, 85, 91,
J.D. Thompson (whaleship),
   96
John Wells (whaleship), 71,
   79-80, 95-96, 99
Julian (whaleship), 101

Kelley, Captain, 102-103
Kohola (whaleship), 105

Lagoda (whaleship), 113-
   114, 117

Massachusetts (whaleship),
   71, 95-96
Mattoon, C.S., 117-120
McGraw, Dr. John, 118
Melville, Herman, 16-18,
   17, 21-22, 28, 42-43

Midas (whaleship), 113-114,
 117
Minerva, 124
Moby Dick, 16-18, 21-22,
 28, 42-43
Monticello (whaleship),
 60, 71-72, 96, 102,
 109, 123
Moses Taylor (steamship),
 117, 120

New Bedford, 15-20, *16*,
 24, 26, 29, 39, 40, 44,
 76, 119, 122, 126-128

Oliver Crocker (whaleship),
 71, 95, 101
Omey, Alexander, 22
Oriole (whaleship), 71, 88,
 122
Owen, Captain, 101

Packard, Captain Timothy
 C., 11-13, 22-23, 25-26,
 27, 29-30, 34-38, 40,
 43, 46-50, 52, 63, 64,
 66-68, 72, 74-75, 79,
 90, 95-96, 102-104,
 109, 118-120, 128
Payne, George, 22
Pease, Captain Henry, 107
Powhattan (merchant ship),
 118

Progress (whaleship), 106,
 113-114, 117

Robinson, Banabas, 23
Roman (whaleship), 96, 98

Schmidt, Paul, 23
Seneca (whaleship), 99
Smith, Captain Elijah, 124
Stivers, John, 22, 25, 27-29,
 39, 41, 45-46, 49, 51-54,
 56-58, 66-67, 83, 89, 91-
 93, 100,109, 118-120, 128
Superior (whaleship), 69

Taber, Gordon & Company,
19, 24, 120
Thomas Dickason, 71, 99

Victoria (whaleship, 105

Williams, Captain Thomas,
 60, 102-103, 123-125, *123*
Williams, Eliza, 60-61
Williams, William Fish,
 109, 115-116
Wood, George, 23